A Curriculum for Personal and Social Education

edited by
Linda Otten

by the Teachers and School Nurse at Piper Hill High School

David Fulton Publishers
London

David Fulton Publishers Ltd
Ormond House, 26–27 Boswell Street, London WC1N 3JD

First published in Great Britain by David Fulton Publishers 1999

The right of Linda Otten to be identified as the editor of this work has been asserted by her in accordance with the Copyright, Designs and Patents Act 1988.

Copyright © David Fulton Publishers 1999

British Library Cataloguing in Publication Data
A catalogue record for this book is available from the British Library

ISBN 1–85346–596–8

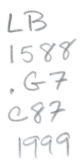

LB
1588
.G7
C87
1999

Typeset by FSH Print & Production Ltd, London
Printed in Great Britain by The Cromwell Press Ltd, Trowbridge, Wilts.

Contents

Acknowledgements v

1 Developing a Personal and Social Education Curriculum 1
About this book – Defining Personal and Social Education –
Piper Hill High School and its community – Aims and philosophy –
The development of the PSE curriculum at Piper Hill –
Organisation, management and coordination of PSE –
Monitoring and evaluation

2 Substance Use and Misuse 15
Use of resources – Training and development –
Medicines (module 1) – Smoking and alcohol (module 2) –
Other substances (module 3)

3 Sex Education 21
A sex education policy – Parental rights of withdrawal –
Using visiting speakers – Confidentiality – School policy on
HIV positive and AIDS – Contraception–the role of the teacher and
the nurse – Sexuality and the acceptance of the individual –
The contents of our Sex Education programme – Body parts
(module 1) – Relationships (module 2) – Life cycles (module 3) –
Public and private (module 4) – Feelings (module 5)

4 Family Life Education 37
Growing up in a family (module 1) – My family and my role in
my family (module 2) – Child development and child care skills
(module 3)

5 Personal Safety 51
Group building activities – Stranger danger (module 1) –
Getting help (module 2) – Living with traffic (module 3)

6 Health Related Exercise   57
Cross-curricular links – Fitness and health (module 1)

7 Food and Nutrition   59
Food Technology at Piper Hill – Issues and attitudes –
Hygiene and safety rules – Healthy eating (module 2) –
Safety in the kitchen (module 3) – Planning and making a simple
meal (module 4) – Breakfast foods (module 6) – Food groups:
vitamins (module 8) – Healthy eating (module 10) – Notes on an
Attitudes to Food workshop

8 Personal Hygiene   75
Certificates – Personal care (module 1) – Showering (module 2) –
Dental care (module 3) – Careers and personal care (module 5) –
Cultural practices in personal hygiene (Muslim)

9 Environmental Aspects of Health Education   91
A balanced healthy lifestyle (module 1) – The spread of diseases
(module 2) – The influence of the media (module 3) – Taking
responsibility (module 4)

10 Advocacy   95
Developing self-esteem – Self-advocacy skills – Citizenship/ASDAN Award
Scheme (module 1) – Skills development throughout the Healthy School
Award (module 2)

11 Independence and Leisure   101
Working towards independence – Independence skills/ASDAN
Award Scheme (module 1) – Leisure activities (module 2) –
Resources and useful addresses

Appendix   Training for Sex Education at Piper Hill   111
Sex education questionnaire – Training for governors –
Training for staff

Bibliography and Resource List   128

Index   131

Acknowledgements

This book is the work of the teachers and the school nurse of Piper Hill High School, Manchester: Jenny Andrews, Janet Ashton, Annie Cubbin, Jane Dowell, Christine Galligan, Anne Glancy, Wendy Godfrey, Linda Jones, Chris Gunstone, Shaheena Hussein, Lesley Josling, Jan Kiely, Jane Lilleyman, Linda Otten, Adrian Thornber, Judy Mapplebeck, Lesley Wood and Kathleen Wood. The work was supported throughout by the Nursery Nurses and Support Workers at Piper Hill, without whose help the developments would not have been possible.

Our thanks to Pat Mason, Police School Liaison Officer, for her contribution to the development of the lessons on Safety; to Cath Fletcher of the Mancunian Health Promotion Specialist Service for her training programme and materials for staff and governor training; to Richard Bridge, Sue Blaylock and Debra Walsh for their secretarial help; and to Colin Collinson for his valuable advice and editing assistance.

The Editor has received a great deal of support, encouragement, training and ideas from the Manchester Healthy School Award Team which includes the Associate Health Education Adviser for Manchester, Elaine Morrison, and Health Promotion Officers Vannesa Brown, Cath Fletcher, Donna Webster, Gareth Adams and Caroline Jackson at the Mancunian Health Promotion Specialist Service.

The Editor acknowledges Piper Hill High School's support for the editing and development of the materials and ideas in this book.

Although this work could not have been possible without the ideas and extensive contributions of the contributing authors, changes have had to be made in the editing process and the editor accepts sole responsibility for any deficiences which may be found.

Chapter 1

Developing a Personal and Social Education Curriculum

About this book

This book is intended for use by teachers of secondary pupils with severe learning disabilities in the Personal and Social Education curriculum. It provides ideas for curriculum content and practical resource materials. It also contains training material to enable a school to provide internal training on Personal and Social Education to be delivered to all staff including support staff. It can be used for a range of purposes: for planning a Personal and Social Education curriculum from start; to develop a specific part of the curriculum, e.g. sex education; to build on a current curriculum; for planning school in service training; and for resources.

This Personal and Social Education curriculum has been written by teachers and the school nurse at Piper Hill High School over the last five years. From our experience of developing this curriculum we offer overall guidance about a framework for Personal and Social Education and about the process of developing a Personal and Social Education curriculum as a whole school. Finding suitable resources can be difficult and time consuming and in this book we suggest a wealth of suitable materials which are linked to each teaching topic.

All the material has been developed and tested by both practising teachers and the school nurse and the authors share their insights and experience and offer a source of extra ideas about delivering the curriculum.

Defining Personal and Social Education

PSE was previously known simply as Health Education, a term still found in older official documents.

Section 1 of the Education Reform Act 1988, restated in paragraphs 331 and 332 of the Education Act 1996, places a statutory responsibility on schools to provide a broad and balanced curriculum which: 'promotes the pupil's spiritual, moral, cultural, mental and physical development; prepares pupils for the opportunities, responsibilities and experiences of adult life'.

At Piper Hill, Personal and Social Education is an essential part of every pupil's curriculum. The curriculum was developed with the specific aims of supporting and promoting attitudes, practices and understanding conducive to good health; fostering social skills, self-esteem and a sense of responsibility.

Education for health begins in the home, where patterns of behaviour and attitudes influence health for good or ill throughout life, and will be established before the child is five. The tasks for schools are to support and promote attitudes, practices and understanding conducive to good health.

> The emphasis schools give to the general care and well-being of pupils in fostering their social skills, self-esteem and sense of responsibility is an essential context for the development of the more organised components of health education. Broadly speaking, these components should be concerned with the provision of knowledge and skills that will enable pupils to understand their own bodies and how to keep them healthy and to have regard for the health of the community. (DES, 1986)

> Health Education cannot be left to chance. While health concerns such as smoking, HIV/ AIDS and personal safety require individual attention, none should be dealt with in isolation. A coherent Health Education programme is required if pupils are to be encouraged to establish healthy patterns of behaviour, to acquire the ability to make healthy choices and to contribute to the development of a healthy population. (NCC, 1990)

> Essential features of health education are the promotion of quality of life and the physical, social and mental well-being of the individual. It covers the provision of information about what is good and what is harmful and involves the development of skills which help individuals to use their knowledge effectively. (NCC, 1990)

Thus PSE is about developing the full potential of every child in order to allow him or her to live a useful, effective and happy life, while considering the needs and promoting the well-being of others. It is concerned with enabling children to make informed choices and decisions in matters relating to their health, by encouraging greater autonomy and feelings of personal worth.

PSE develops an understanding and awareness of the aspects of health for which individuals and groups have some degree of control and responsibility. However, knowledge and information alone are not sufficient: they need to be acquired within a framework of self-awareness and the development of skills. Such skills assist pupils in living and working together in a way that enhances and promotes health within a family, a school, a community or society at large.

About Piper Hill High School and its community

Piper Hill High School is a day secondary school providing education for about 85 pupils who have severe learning disabilities (SLD). About one third of the pupils have profound and multiple learning disabilities (PMLD). There are pupils with a sensory disability (hearing and sight), physical disability and/or challenging behaviour. There is a broad range of ability among these pupils and the curriculum of the school seeks to address this by enabling pupils to access a modified National Curriculum (11–16 years) or a Sensory Curriculum linked to the National Curriculum (11–16 years). From 16–19 years the students follow an FE (Further Education) Curriculum.

Pupils come to Piper Hill when they are 11 years old and stay until the end of the academic year in which they are 19. Most pupils transfer to Piper Hill at the end of Y6 from the linked primary school, The Birches.

The majority of the pupils coming to Piper Hill live in South Manchester (Wythenshawe, Didsbury, Chorlton) and South Central Manchester (Burnage, Withington, Fallowfield and Moss Side), and they attend school on a full time basis. Within school there is a mix of pupils from different ethnic and religious groups as well as from different social and cultural backgrounds.

Piper Hill is situated in a residential area of South Manchester. It has pleasant grounds and has recently undergone a major building programme. Facilities include a hydrotherapy pool, a gym, specialist rooms for science, art, food technology, light and sound stimulation, a soft area, eight general classrooms, a large sensory base, a dining room, a careers room and a flat.

The school has developed good links with the local community. Pupils use the local shops and transport regularly. There are effective links with the local high school and an integration programme is in place.

For the older students, there are links with City College, Manchester, and there is a well-developed transition programme which enables students to start opting into the college courses in preparation for leaving school. Piper Hill also maintains good links with the Wythenshawe Day Resource Centre and a number of students take up places there upon leaving school.

Equal opportunities

We are working at all times to ensure that attitudes of self-esteem and respect are fostered in staff, pupils and their families. The contribution of all pupils, irrespective of background, disability, gender or culture, is valued. All pupils are encouraged to participate fully in the life of the school.

Aims and philosophy

School can have a powerful influence on the development of a healthy lifestyle. Research shows that well planned personal and social education can help to develop positive changes and encourage responsible attitudes and behaviour. At Piper Hill we aim to provide our pupils with accurate information about health education, and to encourage individual responsibility, awareness and informed decision making. For those of our pupils who are not able to manage their own health care we aim to enable them to make choices and provide a high standard of care working closely with parents and carers. We believe our pupils will have the ability to develop a healthy lifestyle if we work in partnership with parents, discussing ideas, planning programmes and carrying out work in cooperation.

Our programme also takes into account the influences of the wider community, peer group and the media on our pupils. We work closely with other health care professionals in school and the community to further our health care aims.

The development of the PSE curriculum at Piper Hill

Sex Education was identified as an area that particularly needed developing at Piper Hill during school staff professional development interviews, and the school management team agreed that Sex Education within the wider scope of the Personal and Social Education curriculum should be a priority on the School Development Plan.

The process

Over a year between 1995/6 the PSE curriculum was developed in the following ways:

- A coordinator for PSE was appointed who was given non-contact time for this work each week.
- The school nurse worked in close partnership with the PSE coordinator.
- A working party was set up consisting of the PSE coordinator, the school nurse, a nursery nurse, a parent governor, a teacher and a head teacher. Regular meetings were held throughout the year.
- All school staff completed a questionnaire about Sex Education at our school (see Appendix).
- Budget money was allotted for resources and training, and resources were purchased.
- The PSE coordinator and the school nurse attended a five-day and a two-day Sex Education training course.
- Two teachers and a nursery nurse attended a one-day training workshop on Sex Education for students with severe and profound learning difficulties.
- The Health Promotion Specialist Service worked with us to develop a and lead staff training. Regular teaching staff training sessions (INSET) were held and a whole days training for all staff including nursery nurses, special school support workers, the speech therapist and the physiotherapy team (see further details in Appendix).
- Governors attended a Sex Education training session and also came to two workshops for parents where our work was demonstrated (see Appendix).
- Teachers each wrote and trialed a section of the Personal and Social Education curriculum, i.e. by dividing up the components (Figure 1.1) between the teachers and allocating time for teachers to write.
- Two workshops were held to consult parents/carers and to show examples of our Sex Education work with students.

At the end of the year a draft PSE curriculum, including Sex Education, was in place and being taught throughout the school. There was an increase in staff confidence shown in teaching and through individual staff annual professional development interviews. The curriculum plan for Years 7–11 is shown in Figure 1.2 and the FE curriculum, Years 12–14 (not covered in this book), in Figure 1.3.

Our curriculum is a working document and since 1996 new chapters have been added on self-Advocacy, Substance Use and Abuse and the ASDAN Award Scheme (explained in Chapter 11).

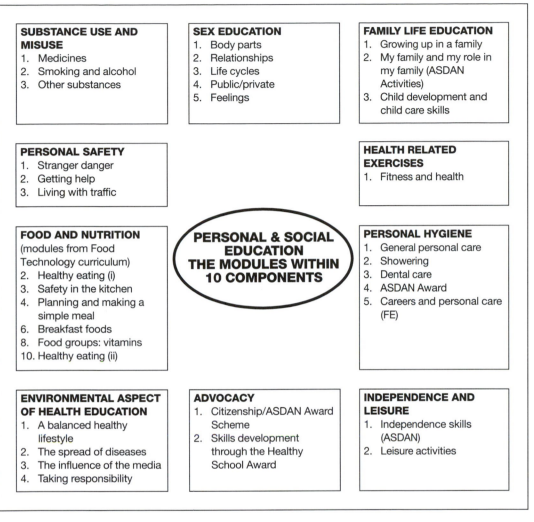

SUBSTANCE USE AND MISUSE
1. Medicines
2. Smoking and alcohol
3. Other substances

SEX EDUCATION
1. Body parts
2. Relationships
3. Life cycles
4. Public/private
5. Feelings

FAMILY LIFE EDUCATION
1. Growing up in a family
2. My family and my role in my family (ASDAN Activities)
3. Child development and child care skills

PERSONAL SAFETY
1. Stranger danger
2. Getting help
3. Living with traffic

HEALTH RELATED EXERCISES
1. Fitness and health

FOOD AND NUTRITION
(modules from Food Technology curriculum)
2. Healthy eating (i)
3. Safety in the kitchen
4. Planning and making a simple meal
6. Breakfast foods
8. Food groups: vitamins
10. Healthy eating (ii)

PERSONAL & SOCIAL EDUCATION THE MODULES WITHIN 10 COMPONENTS

PERSONAL HYGIENE
1. General personal care
2. Showering
3. Dental care
4. ASDAN Award
5. Careers and personal care (FE)

ENVIRONMENTAL ASPECT OF HEALTH EDUCATION
1. A balanced healthy lifestyle
2. The spread of diseases
3. The influence of the media
4. Taking responsibility

ADVOCACY
1. Citizenship/ASDAN Award Scheme
2. Skills development through the Healthy School Award

INDEPENDENCE AND LEISURE
1. Independence skills (ASDAN)
2. Leisure activities

Figure 1.1 Personal and Social Education at Piper Hill High School

Organisation, management and coordination of PSE

Personal and Social Education coordinated by the PSE coordinator, who is responsible for coordinating the work of the teaching team, organising staff training, overall planning and review and ordering resources. The coordinator works closely with the school nurse. A programme of meetings with parents and liaison with the governors is also part of the PSE coordinator's role.

The teacher of the tutor group coordinates the PSE work in his or her tutor group, linking with parents and the health professionals, including the school nurse.

A significant part of lesson time for each pupil not spent on the National Curriculum is used for PSE work.

CURRICULUM PLAN – Years 7–11

	TERM 1	TERM 2	TERM 3
Year 7	Body Parts/ Personal Hygiene	Family Life/ Relationships	Safety/ Life Cycles
Year 8	Health Related Exercise/ Public/Private	Environmental Aspects of Health Education Feelings	Drugs/ Body Parts
Year 9	Personal Hygiene Relationships	Family Life/ Life Cycles	Safety/ Public/Private
Year 10	Family Life ¦ Public/Private ASDAN ACTIVITIES ———→	Life Cycles ¦ Personal ¦ Hygiene	Safety ¦ Feelings
Year 11	Environmental ¦ Body Parts Aspects of ¦ Health ¦ Education ASDAN ACTIVITIES ———→	Family Life and Relationships	Substance ¦ Relationships Use and ¦ and Misuse ¦ Body Parts

Figure 1.2 Curriculum plan, Years 7–11, showing which areas to plan and teach each half term

Delivery and methods

Delivery is in the following ways: tutor group work; whole class teaching; in small groups or individually led by the school nurse or nursery nurse; single sex groups for particular topics; pupils grouped by age, need or ability.

A variety of approaches is used, including drama, group work, individual work, role play, songs, pictures, games, storytelling; and good use is made of models, puppet workshops (Gamlin, 1994) and special videos.

Cross-cultural work

This forms an important part of PSE work, building on our partnership with parents and carers, and with people in the community. Our resources reflect a range of cultural backgrounds, for example traditional dress, Asian food and utensils, and multi-ethnic puppets. Literature on the approaches to health education by different cultures is available in school, and staff training takes account of these issues.

Resources

Resources at Piper Hill are kept in a designated room, where they can be accessed and borrowed by all staff and parents. The Bibliography and Resource List at the end of this book lists a wide range of resources, including health packs, books and videos.

Liaison with primary school

There is liaison with our primary linked school, The Birches, which is being developed through training, discussions, programmes of learning and work with parents. During the pupils' final year at The Birches they follow a transition programme.

Time available for Sex Education and PSE

A proportion of this work is covered in cross-curricular links such as science topics. A large part of the 20 per cent of time not allocated to the National Curriculum is spent on Sex Education and Personal and Social Education.

Who teaches Sex Education?

Designated teachers teach Sex Education, supported by nursery nurses and the school nurse.

Dissemination of the Policy

The Piper Hill School Policy Statement on Sex Education is stated at the beginning of Chapter 3. All teaching staff, the nursing staff and the governors receive a copy of our policy. Teachers make their copy available to class staff. The policy has been fully discussed by governors, parents and all school staff. The statements of moral values, sexuality and acceptance of the individual, and working with parents, were developed at staff training sessions (see Appendix). We felt it was important that our policy grew out of a whole school consultation. After the school nurse and PSE teacher had attended a five-day training course at Manchester University and learnt about important issues, such as legislation and confidentiality, they formed a working party with the head teacher to write the remaining part of the policy. The policy is reviewed each year before it is put in our Piper Hill Staff Handbook.

Progression and continuity in learning

The health education work introduced and learnt by pupils at a earlier age in the primary school is developed and expanded in our programme of learning through visiting topics at regular intervals throughout the pupil's school career (see Figure 1.4, p10). Our work is carefully matched to individual needs based on teacher assessment. As pupils complete work, it is recorded in their own Record of Achievement. Piper Hill's Records of Achievement are in line with Manchester's and also national Records of Achievement. PSE work is continued and developed for students in Years 12–14 in the FE department.

FE CURRICULUM –
Years 12–14

The FE curriculum is a separate document at
Piper Hill High School, and contains Current Affairs,
Citizenship, Careers, Environmental Education,
Leisure and some specific aspects
of Health Education

YEAR 12	TERM 1		TERM 2		TERM 3	
Current Affairs	Local Issues		National Issues		International Issues	
Citizenship	'Our Roots'		Anti-Racism Education		Equality of Opportunity	
Careers	Knowing Me Knowing You	It's Not What You Do...	Dreams Can Come True	Food, Glorious Food	What a job! Workplace Visits	Perfect Individual Careers Interviews
Health Education	Healthy Eating • vitamins • veg. cooking • balance in diet	Environmental Aspects of Health Education: Balanced Healthy Lifestyle	Stay Well (prevention of spread of germs)	First Aid: coping with emergencies	Safety	
Environmental Education	Awareness of need		Study of historical building or archeological site		Improvement and upkeep of school grounds	
	← Improving and conserving the environment: Parrs Wood Environmental Studies Centre →					
PSE/ Leisure	Options in: • drama • music ————————————————————————————→ • art and craft • sport					

Figure 1.3 FE Curriculum, Years 12–14 (not covered in this book)

YEAR 13	TERM 1		TERM 2		TERM 3	
Current Affairs	Producing a school newspaper		How Events Impact on People's Lives		Using the media to promote areas of interest	
Citizenship	My Place in Society		Rules of Society including the Role of the Police		Society, Organisations and our City	
Careers	I'm Too Sexy	Top Hat	Respect Yourself	A Hard Day's Night Really Saying Something	A Hard Day's Night	Money, Money, Money!
Health Education	Sex Education ASDAN Bronze	Personal Hygiene	Sex Education	Personal Hygiene	Independence and Leisure	Healthy Eating ASDAN Bronze Health & Survival
Environmental Education	Community Projects: recycling		← Improving and conserving the environment: Parrs Wood Environmental Studies Centre →			
PSE/ Leisure	**Options in:** • drama • music ————— • art and craft • sport		————————→			

YEAR 14	TERM 1		TERM 2		TERM 3	
Current Affairs	Advertising		← Our Planet → Recycling and Conservation – 'Collective Responsibility'			
Citizenship	Central Government		World Issues		An Ideal World	
Careers	It's My Life	I Want Money	I Will Survive Accidents Will Happen	Independent work experience College Links	Standing for your Rights It's My Life	Moving On Up
Health Education	Family Life in Education	Advocacy	Safety with Medicines – Drugs Education	Environmental Aspects of Health Education	Hobbies and Interests to Promote Good Health	
Environmental Education	Response to Global Environmental Issues		Marketing environmentally friendly products – a local survey ← Improving and conserving the environment: Parrs Wood Environmental Studies Centre →			
PSE/ Leisure	**Options in:** • drama • music ————— • art and craft • sport		————————→			

Figure 1.3 continued

Topics	Year 7	Year 8	Year 9	Year 10	Year 11
Substance Use and Misuse		✓			✓
Family Life Education & Relationships	✓		✓	✓	✓ ✓
Safety	✓		✓	✓	
Food & Nutrition	◄———————————————————————►				
Personal Hygiene	✓		✓	✓	
Health Related Exercise	◄———————————————————————►				
Environmental Aspects of Health Education		✓		✓	
Sex Education					
1. Body Parts	✓	✓			✓ ✓
2. Relationships	✓		✓		✓
3. Life Cycles	✓		✓	✓	
4. Public/Private		✓	✓	✓	
5. Feelings		✓		✓	
Independence & Leisure	◄———————————————————————►				
Advocacy & Enabling	◄———————————————————————►				
ASDAN				◄————————————►	

7. PSE topics plan   *Each box represents half a term

Figure 1.4 Personal and Social Education topic timetable KSs 3 & 4: Years 7–11, for checking each child's progress through the curriculum. Each box represents half a term and the ticks represent the topic which the PSE teacher needs to cover. The squares are coloured when a child completes a topic and so it is clear which topics has covered and needs to revisit.

Monitoring and evaluation

Each pupil's work in PSE is evaluated at the end of each term in a written report. An example of a pupil's Yearly Planning and Review Sheet is given in Figure 1.5. The pupil's annual review contains an evaluation of PSE work throughout the year and is reported to parents/carers. The Review Summary Report contains a statement about any PSE decisions made by teachers and parent/carers at the review,

PSE	Piper Hill High School Yearly Planning & Review Sheet	*Teacher: Year Group:*
		Pupil: 'Lee Jones'

Date	Targets	Date	Evaluation/Assessment
5.9.97	To understand some of his emotions and ways of reacting in specific situations, e.g. being bullied. To build Lee's self-esteem. To understand the basic stages on life cycle.	Dec 97	Lee has particularly enjoyed role playing situations of bullying and has tried some out at break times. He contributes well to discussions. He often gets upset about his friends at school and responds well to talking to a concerned adult. Lee understands the needs of a baby and how to keep it safe. He is aware of sexually appropriate behaviour.
Jan 98	To complete ASDAN challenges for: • Science – hygiene • Family/home – self-advocacy, independent living skills To understand the role of the police		Lee has completed a challenge on hygiene and appropriate behaviour and two challenges on his role in family life. He did an excellent role play and showed that he understood how to liaise with a fellow officer, call for back-up and help at an accident.
April 98	• To write up three ASDAN challenges • To work on ASDAN Personal Autonomy Challenge – asking for help • To understand some rules for Personal Safety and cross a minor road safely	Jan 98	With adult prompts not to rush, he crosses a road safely and has helped to make a road safety video. Although he is good at role playing 'stranger danger', he shows some lack of awareness of the dangers, and he needs to re-visit this topic.

Figure 1.5 Sample of pupil's yearly planning and review sheet

especially noting views on Sex Education. The pupil is also invited to contribute his or her views in a statement to be attached to the Annual Report.

Each teacher's timetable is monitored for allocation of PSE work. For long term evaluation two pupils will be chosen from each year group and their work and progression in PSE monitored over the next few years through records and personal interviews.

Parents and carers are encouraged to contribute to discussions on PSE issues regularly with school staff at coffee mornings and workshops (see Figure 1.7), through home–school books and at individual meetings.

The work and training needs of staff is monitored through yearly professional development interviews, planning development training sessions and questionnaires.

Lesson Plan

Date: 24.6.98   Subject: PSE   Group: 4   Staff:

Learning Objectives:	Activities/Resources
1. To understand the feelings of happiness/ sadness, fright/anger and worry 2. To understand calling for help and who to call 3. To read Paul Plays Football, and how to say 'go away' and telling a teacher	Makaton symbolic feelings sheet Pupils' own video of role play Lisa at the cafe Paul Plays Football, (LDA, 1994) Role play of the story and another similar scenario – time permitting

Key Words/Experiences
> happy/sad
> frightened, angry, calm, worried
> 'come here'/'go away'
> telling Dad – who else could we tell?
> telling a teacher

EVALUATION

Pupils' Names

Figure 1.6 Monitoring and evaluation

Manchester City Council Education Department

Piper Hill High School

200, Yew Tree Lane
Northenden
Manchester M23 0FF

Headteacher:
Jenny Andrews

Tel: 0161 998 4068
Fax: 0161 945 6625

Dear Parents and Carers,

Coffee Morning – Thursday 6th May
11a.m. – 12 noon in Class 7

For some time now your child has been learning about health care, keeping safe, and his or her body.

During the summer term we shall be doing more work on Health and Sex Education and looking at the changes which happen at puberty.

We hope you will read the enclosed Health and Sex Education Plan, and come and talk to us on May 6th at the Coffee Morning and tell us your ideas.

We will have books and materials which we hope to use in our teaching available for you to see.

Best Wishes,

Kathleen Wood
Linda Otten
Karen Bates
Christine Galligan (School Nurse)

Figure 1.7 Encouraging the contribution of parents and carers

Chapter 2

Substance Use and Misuse

At Piper Hill our aims are to increase pupil knowledge and understanding about drugs and related issues both now and in their future lives. Teaching around this topic is closely linked to the development of self-esteem which permeates our whole curriculum at Piper Hill and is also developed through Personal and Social Education. We believe it is important for pupils to develop a range of skills to enable them to make their own informed decisions about drugs and other substances (such as household bleaches and glues).

This chapter refers to the terms substance use and misuse, which is a wider term for drugs education.

Medicines feature because most of our pupils have first hand experience of taking medicines to maintain their health and will need to understand the issues about medicines and their safe use. We refer to a medicine as a substance used for the treatment of illness or disease which is dangerous if used incorrectly – for example, too much paracetamol is extremely dangerous.

Not all drugs are medicinal. Most of our work centres round legal drugs because these relate directly to the pupils' lives, but we also teach about illegal drugs in Module 4 Safety and Substances.

This can be a sensitive area and we remind ourselves of ground rules at the start of a session: usually we make a rule that we do not give information to the group about our family and friends. Recent research and our own experience tells us that drugs' education is most effective when a variety of teaching approaches is used. These are described in this chapter in the selection of teaching plans. We describe a range of techniques to teach pupils about various drugs and medicines including drama and role play, group work, working with visiting professionals, videos, practical demonstrations and shadow puppets.

Use of resources

Recently there has been development of excellent resources in this area namely Story Boards (Headon, 1996) and Drug Pics (Headon, 1998), which are described under module 3.

Shadow puppets are made by cutting shapes from card of cereal packets and then sellotaping a stick to the shape to hold it up (plant sticks are simplest). Puppets are made by the teacher but are so simple that pupils can also make their own. A screen is also needed which can be made from a white sheet either hung from a pole or attached to a square frame. To use the puppets put the screen in front of a window, for a light source, and move the puppets behind the screen. The light shines through the screen and creates a shadow round the puppets. This is a simple and effective way of demonstrating points through characters and objects, e.g. a shadow shape of a child and syringe used in Module 3 Other Substances, stage 2. Drama activities can be used instead of shadow puppets with pupils acting out a situation.

Training and development

Our Personal and Social Education coordinator has had four days of training in Drugs Education and in turn led a teacher In Service Training (INSET) course. More development work is planned for the near future in the use of new resources.

Medicines (module 1)

The various teaching stages that make up module 1 are listed in Figure 2.1. Some possible activities are shown overleaf.

Medicines (module 1)

Stage 1

☐ I know how things can get into my body: through my nose, ears and eyes, e.g. drops and sprays; through my mouth, e.g. medicines
☐ I know how things can get into my body through my lungs, e.g. smoke; through my digestive system, e.g. food; and through my skin into my bloodstream, e.g. germs from a splinter
☐ I understand some ways my body works and how to look after it
☐ I know that some things can harm me and some things are good for my body

Stage 2

☐ I know in more detail how my body works and how to look after it
☐ I know the school rule about medicines, i.e. medicines should be handed to the nurse
☐ I know how medicines can get into our bodies
☐ I know simple safety rules about medicines
☐ I know where medicines come from, e.g. doctor, chemist
☐ I know who to go to for help, e.g. nurse, parent
☐ I know who helps people who are ill

Stage 3

☐ I know in more detail about the way substances can get into our bodies
☐ I know safety rules about medicines: that medicines can be dangerous for young children, and that medicines can be dangerous if taken incorrectly
☐ I know what to do when I am ill and who I can go to in different circumstances, e.g. chemist for travel sickness pills, hospital if I have an accident
☐ I can go to the local chemist with an adult to buy an item, read and understand the label

---

Figure 2.1 Substance use and misuse – the teaching stages for modules 1–3

Smoking and Alcohol (module 2)

Stage 1

☐ I know about smoking and I can distinguish alcohol from soft drinks
☐ I know some of the effects that smoking and alcohol have on my body
☐ I can communicate with others in a group and with adults

Stage 2

☐ I have explored some of the reasons why people smoke and drink
☐ I understand, in more depth, the effects of smoking and alcohol on the body
☐ I have practised decision making and assertiveness
☐ I have explored my feelings and behaviour, in a group, through role play
☐ I know who can help me and how to get help

Stage 3

☐ I know how old I must be to drink alcohol or buy cigarettes
☐ I know safe limits for drinking alcohol
☐ I understand the role of advertising in relation to alcohol and smoking
☐ I understand the words addiction and abuse
☐ I can take responsibility for my own safety and behaviour
☐ I am aware of other people's safety and can give and secure help

Other Substances (module 3)

Stage 1

☐ I know about safety in the home, i.e. the dangers of household cleaning substances
☐ I know about keeping safe in the park and play areas, i.e. what to do if I find a syringe
☐ I know about the uses and dangers from types of glue, aerosols and lighter fuel

Stage 2

☐ I know how to keep myself and others safe at home and in the park or street
☐ I can role play making choices and decision in a group, i.e. what do I do if I am asked to join in glue sniffing in the park
☐ I know who can help me and how to get help, e.g. asking a grown up, talking to the police

Stage 3

☐ I know about the situations when, and the reasons why, people might take other drugs such as cannabis, ecstasy, and amphetamines
☐ I know how to protect myself and others from dangers in the home and community
☐ I can ask the correct adult for help, i.e. using the phone to ring the police

Figure 2.1 continued

Stage 2: I know the school rules on medicines

The concepts are: medicine, asthma, nurse, safety; and the aim is that pupils know the school rules on medicines as stated in their school diary (i.e. that medicines should be handed to the nurse). There are cross-curricular links to English.

☞ **Activity**

Arrange for pupils to visit the medical room for a group session with the school nurse. She talks to them about the importance of keeping drugs safely and why tablets/medicines can be dangerous or helpful.

☞ **Activity**

Pupils look at or read the section in their school diaries about school rules on medicines and then discuss these. Ask who has an asthma inhaler, and why. Where is it?

Words used: asthma, inhaler, medical room, tablets, medicine, safe, dangerous.
Resources: the school nurse, school diary (pupil's personal diary).

Stage 2 and 3: I know simple safety rules about medicines, and who to go to for help

The concepts are: safe/dangerous, tablet, medicine, high up, headache/illness. The aims are that pupils should know when we need medicines, where they come from, and the importance of keeping them safely. There are cross-curricular links with English.

☞ **Activity**

Using shadow puppets (see Use of resources, page 15), the teacher plays two scenarios. In the first, a child is ill with a headache, mum gets a tablet from a bottle on a high shelf and gives it to the child, who starts to feel better. In the second scenario, a child feels ill and goes to get a tablet himself/herself. There the teacher should stop and ask the pupils why this is wrong. Child gets mum. Pupils play the correct situation.

☞ **Activity**

Using shadow puppets, the teacher plays the following scenario. A child is ill. Mum takes the child to a doctor who examines child and gives mum a prescription. Mum then goes to the chemist and gets some medicine, which she gives to the child every day for a week. The child gets better. Pupils play the above.

Words used: headache, tablet, high up, lying down, hot/temperature, doctor, prescription, chemist/chemist's shop, medicine.
Resources: shadow puppet characters: mum, two children, doctor, chemist.

Smoking and alcohol (module 2)

Figure 2.1 shows the teaching stages for module 2, and some suggested activities are given below.

Stage 2: I understand the effects of smoking on the body

The concepts are: the damage smoking does, decision making, peer pressure. The aim is for pupils to understand the effects of smoking on their own bodies and on others, and for them to be able to decide whether to smoke or not, and if not, how to resist pressure.

☞ **Activity**

Put a ball of cotton wool in a plastic bottle and fit a cigarette to the bottle's mouth. Light the cigarette and 'smoke' it by squeezing the bottle. Look at the colour of the cotton wool and discuss. Leave for a week and look again at the cotton wool, smell inside the bottle.

☞ **Activity**

Introduce a video covering the reasons why people start to smoke or choose not to smoke,the effect it has on others and the harmful effect smoking has on our body. We suggest Don't Smoke, You Make me Choke (12 minutes): this has pause points where a teacher can stop for discussion. Follow with role play: pupils are offered a cigarette and explore their feelings (peer pressure) and making a choice.

Words used: body, lungs, smoke, danger, heart, circulation, brain, baby, baby inside mum, under 16, choice, passive smoking.

Resources: cigarettes, cotton wool, plastic bottle, Video *Don't Smoke, You Make me Choke* (Gogglebox, 1996), *Drugs Education – A Practical Guide for Primary School Teachers* – page 19 (Groups in Learning, 1995).

Stage 1: I know some of the effects that alcohol has on the body

The concepts are: alcohol, soft drink. The aims are that pupils understand what alcohol is and its effects on the body.

☞ **Activity**

Present a collection of empty soft drink containers and empty alcohol containers. Let pupils look at these, discuss the differences between them and sort them into categories. Then ask pupils to choose a drinks container and discuss the type of drink and the effect it has on their body.

Words used: drinks container, soft drink, alcohol.
Resources: various drinks containers.

Other substances (module 3)

The teaching stages for this module are shown in Figure 2.1.

Stage 1: I know about keeping safe in the park and play areas – what to do if I find a syringe

The concepts are: syringe/needle, help, safe/danger, germs/virus. The aim is that pupils know what to to do if they find a syringe. There are cross-curricular links with English.

☞ **Activity**

Using the shadow puppets, the teacher plays the scenario of children finding a syringe on the ground in the park. (Stop – ask pupils what to do: DO NOT TOUCH.) They fetch mum who sweeps it up with a dustpan and brush and puts it in a used can. She rings the Town Hall, Environmental Health Department. Later that day the Environmental Health Officer comes in his van to collect the syringe in the can. Now let the pupils operate the puppets and tell the story to see if they have understood what to do if a syringe is found.

Words used: syringe, needle, danger, germs/virus, town hall, van, telephone (number on leaflet), do not touch.
Resources: leaflet on needle disposal (with Environmental Health telephone number). Shadow puppets: mum, two children, syringe, can, dustpan, telephone, van.

Stage 1: I know about the uses and dangers of different types of glue, aerosols and lighter fuel

The concepts are glue, aerosol. The aim is that pupils understand the dangers of trying glue sniffing.

☞ **Activity**

Use a laminated drawing of types of glue (Drug Pics resource) which has space for written captions and also matching worksheets. The teacher discusses the uses and dangers of glues, and the class compose captions which the teacher writes up for display. Pupils also fill in their own worksheets.

Words used: glue, stick, sniff, safe/dangerous, breathing – stop, heart – stop.
Resources: Drug Pics (Headon, 1998).

Stage 2: I know what to do if I am asked to join in glue sniffing in the park

The concepts are: choice, help. The aim is to enable pupils to make choices and decisions in a group.

☞ **Activity**

Use two large laminated boards depicting a school building and grounds or park (Story Board resource), plus smaller laminated figures of people and objects (glue). Let the pupils choose a figure and become that character. They then role play a scene where glue is sniffed, and possible (safe) outcomes.

Words used: come on, have a go, plastic bag, ill, okay/no, somebody is sniffing glue.
Resources: Story Boards (Headon, 1996), and figures and objects (which can be custom made).

Stage 3: I know safe limits for drinking alcohol

The concepts are: drinking and driving, alcohol and crime. The aims are that pupils are aware of safe limits for drinking alcohol, of the laws on alcohol, and where to go for help.

☞ **Activity**

Show a video such as Think Before you Drink using the pause button so that pupils can discuss important points (why people drink, the effect of drink on the body, the law on alcohol, and getting help). Alternatively, invite a Police School Liaison Officer to work with the pupils to explore the effects of drinking and driving. The Officer could show an intoximeter and explain its use in measuring how much has been drunk, the dangers of drinking and driving, and links between alcohol and crime.

Words used: alcohol, good, bad, brain, stomach, heart, celebration, problem, need, feelings, relaxed, happy, sad, alone, adult, crime.
Resources: video such as *Think Before you Drink* (Gogglebox, 1996); Police School Liaison Officer.

Chapter 3

Sex Education

A sex education policy

At Piper Hill, we aim to work in an atmosphere of trust and tolerance with all members of the school community.

Our programme of Sex Education has been planned to meet pupils' differing needs and abilities and to help them develop awareness of their bodies and emotions, approaching the choices they have to make with self-esteem, confidence and consideration for others. We acknowledge that the home–school partnership is essential to provide a consistent approach to sex education, and we aim to work together so that steps can be taken to address each pupil's needs.

It is important that parents and carers are well informed and understand the issues around sexuality – for example, the importance of self-esteem and personal relationships. We have always involved parents in the development of our sex education policy; they are invited to coffee mornings and workshops on sex education, and we encourage discussion at formal meetings such as reviews and also informally as matters arise. Parents can see sex and health education resources on these occasions, or at other times by contacting the teacher/tutor. Those resources which are kept in the resources room may be used to develop skills and common understanding between school and home.

The school also works with other professionals such as the local MENCAP Unit, the school nurse and doctors to build up supportive networks and information.

Training for those involved in sex education is essential and some information about how this is handled at Piper Hill is given in the Appendix.

Parental rights of withdrawal

Parents have the right to withdraw pupils from all or part of sex education that does not form part of the statutory National Curriculum. HIV, AIDS, sexually transmitted diseases and non-biological aspects of sexual behaviour have been removed from the National Curriculum, and these are now part of a distinct sex education programme which must be offered, but from which parents have a right to withdraw their children. However, the right of withdrawal does not include students over compulsory school age; nor can parents withdraw pupils from sex education included within other National Curriculum subjects such as science.

If a parent has withdrawn a pupil from a non-statutory sex education programme, a teacher may not give advice to that pupil on sexual matters without parental consent. However, a teacher suggesting where a child might seek confidential information – for example, from their GP, the Brook Advisory Centre or a specialised clinic – is not deemed to be providing sex education, but merely giving information as to where advice, counselling (and treatment) could lawfully be obtained. As a general rule, teachers are not qualified to give medical advice to pupils and should refer them for such advice to a medical professional.

Parents should be informed about which aspects of sex education it is possible to withdraw pupils from and which it is not. Requests for a pupil to be withdrawn from the sex education programme by a parent or carer can be made in a verbal or written form, but a verbal request should be recorded in writing by the school.

Reasons for withdrawal do not need to be given, but the teacher should discuss the nature of the parent or carer's concern and see if they can be reassured. If the parents are not reassured and still wish to exercise their right of withdrawal teachers should explore whether a pupil is to be withdrawn from all or part of the programme, and specify which part. It is important that pupils who are withdrawn should not have other elements of their education disrupted, or be caused the least embarrassment or disruption to their programme of learning.

Once a request that a child be withdrawn has been made, that request must be complied with until the parent or carer changes or revokes it.

All these points are incorporated into Piper Hill's policy statement, a copy of which we make available to parents on request. In addition, parents and carers are able to borrow materials from our school to use in sex education at home.

Using visiting speakers

The use of suitably qualified and experienced outside visitors can enhance the school sex education programme. Visiting speakers should be given a copy of the school sex education policy and be made aware of the school ethos and the way sex education is being delivered. We always use our visiting speakers as part of a planned programme, which will include follow up work, and they are always fully supported by a member of the teaching staff, especially when working with children and students.

Confidentiality

Where the well-being and protection of pupils is concerned there can be no concept of complete confidentiality. If a member of staff is told something which they feel concerned about they should discuss it with the head teacher, who will decide what action to take. Pupils cannot expect that the information they give will not be acted upon. It is inadvisable to question a pupil closely after a disclosure – this may do more harm than good. At Piper Hill, the Child Protection Guidelines are written into our Staff Handbook (based on Manchester City Council Guidelines), and schools may wish to check that their own Guidelines (based on their own local authority) are likewise clearly set out for staff.

School policy on HIV positive and AIDS

There is no need for every school to have a stated policy on HIV positive and AIDS. We reviewed ours in July 1996 and adopted the following policy of confidentiality, written by the Manchester City Council. It applies to all employed at Piper Hill: pupils who are HIV positive or have AIDS are also entitled to be treated in a confidential manner.

> *Manchester City Council – AIDS Policy: Confidentiality*
> *Approved by the Health Subcommittee October 1987*
> The Council as a whole has an existing requirement concerning confidentiality. All information, particularly personal health information, held in pursuance of Council services or employees, is confidential and must be kept so. This is a general duty that already exists. This means that information may only be communicated to another individual or employee if that person has a legitimate need to know in pursuance of their duties and responsibilities as an employee.
>
> The overall principles defining 'legitimate need to know' are:
>
> For clients, that it arises from their request or need for a service and, other than exceptional circumstances, their permission must be obtained before the information is shared.
>
> For employees, it will relate to the Council's general duty of care including health and safety, and its service responsibilities. (Manchester City Council, 1998).

General precautions

To avoid unnecessary contact with any infectious virus disposable rubber gloves should always be worn when changing pupils, administering first aid, treating open wounds, cleaning pupils' teeth. Open wounds should be covered with waterproof elastoplast.

There is am extremely limited risk of becoming HIV positive by day to day contact with anyone carrying the virus in the school situation. Remember, wearing rubber gloves also prevents you passing on any infections to the individuals you are assisting.

Contraception – the role of the teacher and the nurse

First it is important to remember what teachers can and cannot do. They can provide education about types of contraception and where these may be obtained, to all pupils receiving Sex Education. They can provide all pupils with information about where, and from whom, confidential advice and treatment may be obtained. But teachers are not medical professionals and it would be inappropriate for a teacher to give detailed medical advice. However, advice about contraception forms part of the statutory sex education programme, whether given on a one-to-one basis or in a group. Pupils who have been withdrawn from this programme may not be given such advice although, as stated earlier, information regarding sources of confidential advice and treatment does not count as sex education, and can be made freely available to all pupils.

In addition to the role of the teacher, we have a school nurse available for confidential advice on sexual health including contraception. She aims to meet the needs of individual students by providing support and information liaising with the school doctor where appropriate. Every pupil has a medical at least every two years, and this can provide the opportunity for discussion, advice for parents, and support for the pupil.

Sexuality and the acceptance of the individual

In our school the governing body, in consultation with the head and teaching staff, has decided the content of the sex education programme and endeavours to ensure that the needs of all pupils are met. Research suggests that many lesbians and gay men felt unsupported by the school sex education they received, and experienced isolation during their time at school.

Thus one of our aims is to ensure that everyone feels accepted for who they are, including their sexuality and sexual orientation: we value the uniqueness of each individual.

The contents of our Sex Education programme

Our Sex Education programme is planned in five modules: Body parts; Relationships; Life cycles; Public/private; and Feelings. More details are shown in Figure 3.1.

It is important to recognise that this programme, as with other areas of the curriculum, is carried out and developed as the students move through the FE Department (Years 12-14). Many pupils in Key Stages 3 and 4 will cover only the early teaching stages. Those involved in teaching sex education are recommended to read *Sex in Context* (Downs and Craft, 1997) and *Let's Do It* (Scott *et al.*, 1997), which both contain very helpful advice on teaching about sensitive areas, such as masturbation.

The teaching stages within each module are now outlined, and some of the activities we use to teach various stages are briefly described.

Body parts (module 1)

At each stage of this module pupils will develop their self-esteem and be encouraged to value their body. The teaching stages are:
- ☐ I know what my body can do.
- ☐ I am aware of others' bodies: I know some similarities and differences between the sexes.
- ☐ I understand growth and body changes at puberty.
- ☐ I can cope with the changes at puberty.
- ☐ I understand the functions of sexual body parts.
- ☐ I understand the functions of sexual body parts in more detail and depth.
- ☐ I understand conception, pregnancy and birth.
- ☐ I know about contraception, pregnancy and sexual health.

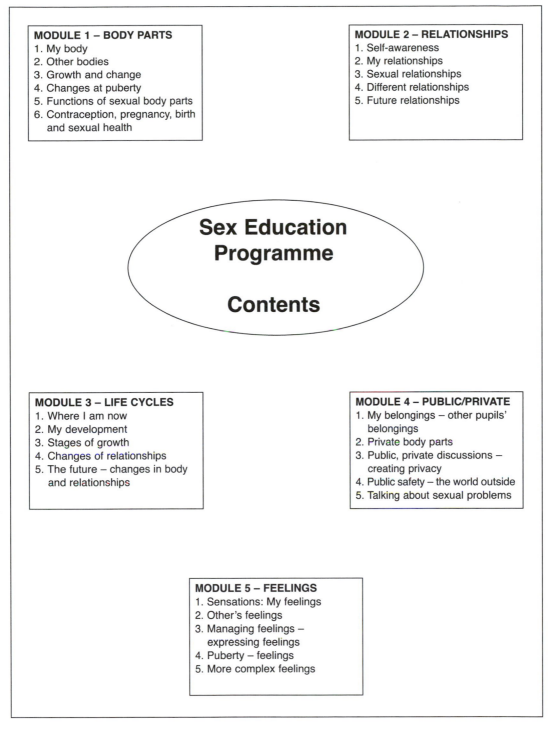

MODULE 1 – BODY PARTS
1. My body
2. Other bodies
3. Growth and change
4. Changes at puberty
5. Functions of sexual body parts
6. Contraception, pregnancy, birth and sexual health

MODULE 2 – RELATIONSHIPS
1. Self-awareness
2. My relationships
3. Sexual relationships
4. Different relationships
5. Future relationships

Sex Education Programme

Contents

MODULE 3 – LIFE CYCLES
1. Where I am now
2. My development
3. Stages of growth
4. Changes of relationships
5. The future – changes in body and relationships

MODULE 4 – PUBLIC/PRIVATE
1. My belongings – other pupils' belongings
2. Private body parts
3. Public, private discussions – creating privacy
4. Public safety – the world outside
5. Talking about sexual problems

MODULE 5 – FEELINGS
1. Sensations: My feelings
2. Other's feelings
3. Managing feelings – expressing feelings
4. Puberty – feelings
5. More complex feelings

Figure 3.1 The Sex Education programme at Piper Hill High School; adapted from Scott et al. (1994) p91

Stage 1: I know what my body can do

The concepts here are: myself, my activities; the aims are to build self-esteem and to make pupils aware of their own bodies and functions. There are cross-curricular links to Relationships (module 2) Stage 1, Life Cycles (module 3) Stage 1, and language work (English).

☞ **Activity**

Link with music and movement in PE so that pupils experience movement and use the parts of the body. As each pupil develops awareness of his or her body, photograph the activities for their Record of Achievement, with a suitable caption, e.g. I can climb along a bench using my legs.

☞ **Activity**

Group games. In the first game, each pupil performs an action in turn which is described (e.g. 'Jamie can jump' or 'I can jump'). In the second game, the group passes the cushion using different parts of the body.

Words used: eat, drink, sneeze, yawn, clap etc. depending on pupils' physical ability.
Resources: pictures and words of various activities, e.g. jumping, running; Communication Passports (containing a photo and all the essential information about a pupil with PMLD which anyone new meeting them would need to know and made up by Piper Hill staff) – see p30; *On the Agenda* (Scott *et al.*, 1994) – the cushion game is described on p23.

Stage 2: I am aware of others' bodies. I know some similarities and differences between the sexes

The main concepts are: male/female, same/different, and the aims are that pupils recognise that there are both male and female, and that other people may be different from themselves. There are cross-curricular links to Life Cycles (module 3) Stages 1 and 2.

☞ **Activity**

In this activity pupils learn to identify themselves and their sex (e.g. 'I am Susan, I am a girl/woman'). Use this to divide the group into male and female. Have a pile of objects associated predominantly with one or other sex (e.g. shaving foam, hair ribbon, necklace, razor) and get the pupils to choose which items belong to which group.

☞ **Activity**

Sorting games: Using a box of assorted male/female clothing, organise a clothes sorting game. For example, the teacher might say 'choose something which goes around a man's neck' and pupil should choose a tie from the box (see Scott et al., 1994, p137). Other suitable games are the 'all change' circle game (e.g. all those with blue eyes change places); and sorting age-appropriate objects (e.g. a lipstick, shaving cream, a cuddly toy) and answer the teacher's question 'who would use this?'

Words used: older/younger, male/female, same/different, boy/girl, man/woman, toddler, grown up.

Resources: collection of male and female objects; collection of age appropriate objects; *On the Agenda* (Scott *et al.*, 1994, pp138–139).

Stages 3 and 4: I understand growth and body changes at puberty. I can cope with changes

The main concept is: change and development, and the aim is to make pupils aware of changes that will happen to their bodies and understand how to cope with these changes. There are cross-curricular links with Life Cycles (module 3) Stages 1,2 and 3, and all stages of Feelings (module 5).

☞ **Activity**
Introduce the pupils to male and female cloth models and encourage observation. Together, look at line drawings of girls and boys at different stages of growth and discuss changes at puberty. Using basic line drawings of bodies, get the students to draw in changes at puberty. Repeat for the opposite sex.

☞ **Activity**
This activity is taught to those who are ready in a 'boys only' group. Pupils look at line drawings of a wet dream and discuss what happens, why it happens and what does the person feel.

Words used: hair, chest, under-arm, beard, shave, penis/willy, semen/spunk, testicles/balls, breasts, pubic hair, muscles, shape, voice, bra, periods.

Resources: male and female cloth models (Brook Advisory Centre, 1990); *Learning to Love series* (Fraser, 1997); *Living Your Life* worksheets 10–17 (Craft, 1991) have a series of line drawings which may be useful here.

Stage 4 : I can cope with my periods

The concepts are: pads, periods, a month, who to tell. The aims are that pupils understand what happens during a period, and learn how to change a pad and ask for help.

☞ **Activity**
This is a 'girl's only' activity (note that boys do learn about menstruation, but in a different way). Use a suitable worksheet pack and work through sheets with pupils individually or in a small group. (Piper Hill's own Growing up teaching pack includes drawings of a girl growing up and a place where the pupil can draw or fill in her own information. The pack was written by the school nurse.) Watch and discuss the video *Janet's got her Period*.

☞ **Activity**
Practise putting a clean pad on pants; discuss where to throw soiled pads and how to change pads. Talk about who pupils can ask for help.

Words used: period, bin, blood, change, dirty/clean, sanitary pad/towel, vagina, vulva, menstruation.

Resources: worksheets (possibly custom-made); the video *Janet's got her Period* (Boulton Hawker Films, 1990).

Stage 4 : I understand masturbation

The concept is: male and female masturbation. The aims are that pupils recognise feelings attached to sexual activity and understand what masturbation is, and its appropriate place, and to reinforce the concept of appropriate private space. There are cross-curricular links to Public/Private (module 4).

☞ **Activity**

Working in single sex groups, identify physical sensations that occur in the body when physical activity takes place. Pupils run on the spot or dance for two minutes, then sit down and notice changes which have taken place in their bodies, e.g. feeling hot and sweaty with a faster heartbeat (see Scott, et al. 1997, p91 for a fuller description). The activity may then be fuller developed by following 'The Masturbation Story' (op.cit. pp109–112) which is a story using models to give pupils information.

☞ **Activity**

Show the video Piece by Piece which shows the puppets masturbating in privacy. (NB Teachers must watch the video themselves before planning this activity.) After viewing the video, allow time for group discussion, focusing on the puppets and remembering to use distancing teaching techniques – that is, no pupil or adult needs to discuss themselves personally.

Words used: sexy, erection, ejaculation, orgasm/come, semen, vagina, clitoris. Page 21 of the *Piece by Piece* guidance notes has a useful list of commonly used words.
Resources: *Let's Do It*, p11 and p109; (Scott *et al.*, 1997) *Piece by Piece* – video and guidance notes pack (Pavilion, 1996).

Stage 5: I understand the functions of sexual body parts

The concept is: growth and change. The aims are for pupils to understand some functions of sexual body parts, and to understand functions in more depth.

☞ **Activity**

Arrange for pupils to watch a baby being breast-fed either by inviting a breast feeding mother into school or organising a visit to the local clinic to see feeding. Use Living Your Life worksheets 10–17 (which are drawings of male and female bodies) to identify sexual body parts. Identify external parts on male and female cloth models.

☞ **Activity**

Discuss how diagrams of our insides are made. Using first an example of an orange cut open to see the fruit inside, introduce a body model from the Health Promotion Unit. Books like The Amazing Pull-out Pop-up Body in a Book which shows organs as 'pop-ups' are useful for extending awareness.

Words used: breasts/nipples, willy/penis, testicles/balls, spunk/semen, wee-hole/urethra, poo-hole/anus, baby-making hole/vagina, womb.
Resources: male and female cloth models; model of a torso – Health Promotion Unit; *Living Your Life* (Craft, 1991); *Learning to Love* (Fraser, 1997), *How a Baby Starts*; *The Amazing Pull-out Pop-up Body in a Book* (Hawcock, 1997).

Stage 6: I know about contraception and sexual health; I understand how to use a condom

The concepts are: contraception, safe sex. The aim is that pupils understand why a condom is used.

☞ **Activity**
Watch the video Piece by Piece Section 5 – or similar material – showing the use of a condom. Let them also watch My Choice, My Own Choice, showing how to use a condom.

☞ **Activity**
Practise putting a condom on a plastic model, using a selection of different condoms. The booklet Contraception (Fraser, 1997, p12) is helpful reading.

Words used: condom, sheath (and other words the pupils may know, e.g. johnny, rubber, french letter), penis, hard, semen, roll.
Resources: the videos *Piece by Piece* (Pavilion, 1996) and *My Choice, My Own Choice* (Clarke, 1992); plastic model for practising putting on a condom (available from Durex); a selection of different condoms; *Contraception* (Fraser, 1997).

Stage 6: I know about sexual health; I can protect myself against sexually transmitted diseases (STDs)

The concept is: sexually transmitted infections. The aim is that pupils understand how to keep safe from sexual infections.

☞ **Activity**
Talk about how to keep the sexual organs clean. The book Sex, Health and Infections (Fraser, 1997) is useful reading; pages 12–13 for cleanliness, and pages 14–16 to promote talk about what is not healthy. Link with the lesson on condoms.

☞ **Activity**
Arrange a visit to a genito-urinary medicine clinic (GUM) so that pupils can talk to the nurses there. At this point, liaison with the school nurse is important.

Words used: safe, safe sex, disease, infection, HIV, confidential (private), bacteria, virus, parasite, fungus, sore, blister, urine, penis, vagina, pain, discharge, clinic, STD
Resources: school nurse, GUM clinic, Young Person's Family Planning Clinic and nurses.

Relationships (module 2)

The teaching stages for this module are as follows:
   ☐ I have developed self-awareness.
   ☐ I understand my relationships in my particular family: I can explain them using the correct vocabulary.
   ☐ I can talk about my friendships and understand some of the ways my friendships are made, change and develop.

☐ I have learnt something about the nature of sexual relationships.
☐ I understand that people form different relationships.

Stage 1: I have developed self-awareness

The concept is myself. The aim is for the pupil to know what is special to him or her. There are cross-curricular links with English: communication, writing and reading; the RE curriculum.

☞ **Activity**
SLD pupils are helped to make a book about 'Myself', recording interests, likes and dislikes. PMLD pupils are helped to make and use a Communication Passport (outlined on p26).

☞ **Activity**
Pupils are encouraged to record and read about themselves at school using a Record of Achievement (see also p7 and p26). Play the circle game with pupils introducing themselves and making a simple statement – for example 'I am Jane and I like swimming'. Or organise an adult to introduce the child.

Words used: I like; my/mine. Individual word lists of interests, toys and activities.
Resources: Communication Passports and Records of Achievement (pupils' own recording documents).

Stage 3: I have learned something about the nature of sexual relationships

Concepts are: the nature of a sexual relationship; what can happen; what is okay for me; saying 'no'; saying 'yes'. The aims are that pupils understand what can happen in a sexual relationship, that they are able to identify feelings about specific behaviour, and understand appropriate responses. There are cross-curricular links to the Body parts and Feelings modules.

☞ **Activity**
In a group watch the disco scenes from the video Piece by Piece and discuss feelings and appropriate behaviour.

☞ **Activity**
Use male and female models to role play and discuss appropriate behaviour using the video as a starting point.

Words used: shaking hands, hug, kiss, saying 'no – I don't like it', enjoying, happy, touching.
Resources: *Piece by Piece* video and guidance notes pack (Pavilion, 1996).

Stage 5: Future relationships

The aims are to learn about and discuss the possibilities of a sexual relationship.

☞ **Activity**
Use the video from My Choice, My Own Choice (Clarke, 1992), watching it over a period of several weeks and following the plan in teacher's pack.

Resources: teachers' booklet and video: *My Choice, My Own Choice* (Clarke, 1992).

Life cycles (module 3)

The teaching stages for this module are as follows:
☐ I know where I am now.
☐ I understand how I developed to this point.
☐ I know what a person can do at each stage of growth.
☐ I know about family relationships.
☐ I know these can change at each stage of life.
☐ I know who I might become and what my future body changes might be.
☐ I understand changes in status in relationships.

Stage 2: I understand how I developed to this point

The concepts are: baby, toddler, child and growth, and the aims are that pupils understand that they have changed and are aware of what they used to be like. There are cross-curricular links with the history curriculum.

☞ **Activity**
Get the pupils to collect photos of themselves as a baby, toddler and young child, and now; have them arrange these in a sequence. Use this as a basis to discuss their development to the present time.

☞ **Activity**
Collect toys and objects used by a baby and a toddler; discuss with the pupils which things they liked and needed, and why.

Words used: baby, toddler, bigger, taller, myself, when I was…, now I can…
Resources: photos, collections of toys.

Stage 3: I know what a person can do at each stage of growth

The concepts are: growth, change and development, and the aim is to learn about the basic stages of life, and what each person can do and needs at each stage. There are cross-curricular links with Body parts, module 1 of this programme.

☞ **Activity**
Organise a visit to a baby clinic to learn about a baby's needs and care. Watch a baby with his or her mother and also a toddler and discuss the differences in the interaction.

☞ **Activity**
Look at line drawings showing growth from babyhood to adult; discuss the changes and make a book of the sequence (using cut-outs of drawings). Act scenes from a baby's, toddler's, teenager's and old person's life – for instance a teenager listening to pop music – using simple home-made puppets.

Words used: baby, toddler, child, teenager, grown up, woman/man, old person.
Resources: *Living Your Life* (Croft, 1991) for line drawings at each stage of development; puppets made by pupils.

Public and private (module 4)

The teaching stages for this module are as follows:

☐ I know which are my belongings and things I can use which belong to other people.

☐ I can name body parts which are private (sexual).

☐ I know what I can talk about, when, and which language to use (e.g. for various body functions).

☐ I know who I can talk to and how to behave in public.

☐ I know when I need privacy and how to create it at home and at school.

☐ I know how to behave at school, at home and in the community.

☐ I know what is safe for me in public places, such as places where I undress, e.g. swimming bath, public toilets.

☐ I can transfer my knowledge to other situations, e.g. college.

☐ I know who I can talk to about specific things, e.g. sexual health problems.

Throughout, teachers need to be sensitive to particular cultural practices – for instance, in the Muslim culture there are particular requirements relating to cleanliness and toileting, and also to modesty of dress, which are part of the Islamic faith (see also Chapter 8).

Stage 1: I know which are my belongings, and I know some things I can use which belong to other people.

The concepts are: my things, others' belongings.; and the aims are that pupils understand which are their own possessions and which things they can share or borrow. There are cross-curricular links to PSE Personal Hygiene.

☞ **Activity**

Give each pupil a sheet of paper headed 'My Things' and ask them to draw or find pictures of their own possessions to stick on to the sheet. Photos of the pupils' possessions would be ideal.

Extend the activity by giving each pupil a sheet of paper headed 'Other People's Things I Use' and, starting with school items, the pupil draws or sticks photos of things he or she uses on to the sheet.

☞ **Activity**

Use the song: 'Mary wore her red dress' (This Little Puffin, p.166).

Form the children in a circle and, choosing an item of clothing for each child sing the song around the circle.

Words used: my and mine, you and yours, other people's, toothbrush, brush, names of clothes and toys; *This Little Puffin* (Matterson, 1969)..

Resources: photographs of pupils' possessions; catalogues with pictures of clothes and toys.

Stage 2: I can name body parts which are private

The concepts are: idea of male/female, knowledge of some body parts and functions. The aims are to name sexual body parts, and to create a 'safe' group in a private place. There are cross-curricular links to science.

☞ **Activity**
Look at pictures and drawings of sexual body parts and encourage the children to give you the names they know for sexual parts of the body. Decide within the group which names will be used.

☞ **Activity**
Using a 'blank' line drawing of the body of a male and female person, get the pupils to put in the sexual parts.

Words used: breasts, nipple, wee hole, vagina, penis, willy, testicles, balls, poo-hole, anus.
Resources: *Living Your Life* (Craft, 1991) teacher's handbook and photocopiable sheets of line drawings.

Stage 3: I know what I can talk about, when, and which language I use. I know who to talk to and how to behave in public.

The concepts are: coping with periods, and the need for privacy (when using the toilet and undressing and dressing). The aims are to develop appropriate behaviour when talking about private body functions, and to learn how to behave in public. There are cross-curricular links to Body parts, Life cycles, and Feelings (modules 1, 3 and 5 of this programme).

☞ **Activity**
Use colour photos and illustrations to discuss with the pupils what behaviours are appropriate in public and what in private. Materials in Picture yourself Set 2 (Craft and Dixon, 1992) may be useful here.

☞ **Activity**
Use a collection of clothing including outerwear and underwear and ask pupils to sort these by placing items either in an open basket or a box marked 'private', depending on whether the clothes are private or ones we show to others. There is a version of this game described in On the Agenda (p137). Let's Do It also contains a series of games to reinforce the idea of public and private.

☞ **Activity**
Discuss with pupils what behaviour is appropriate in public – i.e. in school and on visits in the community – and establish with them some clear rules. For instance, that pupils' privacy is respected when changing clothes and going to the toilet by keeping doors closed, and that there should be consideration for others by flushing the toilet and so on. Teachers will need to prepare in advance for this by discussing parents' concerns with them, so that common aims are developed.

Words used: toilet, private, pad, shut/open, wee, poo, toilet paper, flush toilet, bin.
Resources: collection of clothing, outerwear and underwear; *On the Agenda* (Scott *et al.*, 1994); *Let's Do It* (Scott *et al.*, 1997); photos of public and private places, such as a bedroom, a supermarket.

Stage 3: I know when I need privacy and how to create it at home and school

The concept is private, public; and the aim is that pupils learn to behave appropriately at school and in public (e.g. on school visits). There are cross-curricular links to Stranger Danger module of Personal Safety (Chapter 5)..

☞ Activity

Promote a discussion of what you can do where, using photos of different places. The colour photos on Set 2 of Picture yourself (Craft and Dixon, 1992) are useful here. The concept can be reinforced with 'a public, private' mime game such as those in On the Agenda (p144) and Let's Do It (section 4). The teacher builds a private space in the room, e.g. a bookcase which is large enough to hide behind. The teacher then gives the pupil an activity to mime. If the pupil thinks it should be done in private then he or she mimes it in the private space – for instance, going to the toilet. If the pupil thinks it is public then it is mimed for the class – for instance, eating an apple.

☞ Activity

Use various methods for teaching appropriate behaviour in school for creating own personal space, using toilets and changing. For example: planning individual pupil targets; acting out situations, practising, for example, correct ways to greet people; using the video Janet's got her Period to demonstrate appropriate handling of periods.

Words used: private, mime, pretend.
Resources: *Picture yourself* (Craft and Dixon, 1992); *On the Agenda* (Scott *et al.*, 1994); *Let's Do It* (Scott *et al.*, 1997); *Janet's got her Period* (Boulton Hawker Films, 1990); *Living Your Life* (Craft, 1991).

Stage 3: If I want to masturbate, where can I do it?

The concepts are: erection, masturbation, climax – coming, and the aim is to understand the way to create privacy for masturbation. There are cross-curricular links to Body Parts (module 1, stage 4) and Feelings (module 5, stages 4 and 5) of this programme.

☞ Activity

Initiate discussions on male masturbation (Picture Yourself cards Set 4 42–48 and Living Your Life) and female masturbation (Picture yourself cards Set 4 36–41). Look at the sequence and discuss why the person might be doing this, what happens, and where it happens. Watch the video Piece by Piece and discuss. (It is important that teachers view this themselves in advance.)

☞ Activity

The following is a single sex group activity. Use a shadow puppet or cloth model (male or female, to fit the group, plus props for door and bed) to create a scenario for masturbation. Open up discussion:

Where does the puppet go? What is happening? Why is this man/woman (young person) doing this? Where does he/she do it? Emphasising shutting the bedroom door.

Words used: private, shut the door, penis, willy, vulva, rub, climax, come.
Resources: *Picture yourself* (Craft and Dixon, 1992); *Living Your Life* (Craft, 1991); *Piece by Piece* (Pavilion, 1996); shadow puppets or cloth male or female models (e.g. Brook Advisory Centre, 1990); *Sex in Context* (Downs and Craft, 1997) – the adult training section contains valuable advice on the implications of this topic.

Feelings (module 5)

The teaching stages for this module are as follows:
- ☐ I experience a variety of sensations.
- ☐ I can recognise some of my own feelings, e.g. use of body language, and words such as I'm happy, sad, fed up, hurt, frightened, angry, tired.
- ☐ I have my feelings recognised by an adult.
- ☐ I can recognise some feelings in other people.
- ☐ I can manage some of my feelings.
- ☐ I can express more complex feelings like pleasure, shyness, boredom and feeling left out.
- ☐ I understand adolescence and the growth which takes place.
- ☐ I know how I feel and I can manage these feelings.
- ☐ I understand more complex feelings: jealousy, nervousness, surprise and worry.
- ☐ I understand feelings which may be related to disability, gender, race and power.

Stage 1: I experience a variety of sensations; I have a feeling acknowledged by an adult

The concepts are: musical and tactile sensations, involvement in a group, and the aim is to establish a group feeling and give pupils the opportunity to relate to one another.

☞ **Activity**
'Hello' chant: Pupils' names are repeated to a rhythm on a drum. As each pupil's name is chanted, he or she holds a balloon filled with some lentils, which is then passed on to the next pupil whose name is chanted. This can be followed by the pupils holding on to a large thick circle of elastic and chanting all the names in the group. This helps the feeling of belonging to the group.

☞ **Activity**
Let the pupils listen to two types of music, then the teacher reflects their response. For instance, 'You look happy, Nur, you enjoyed that' or 'You look upset, Alan, was that too loud?'

Words used: names of pupils, beaten on drum.
Resources: musical instruments, elastic circle, balloon filled with lentils. *On the Agenda* (Scott *et al.*, 1994); *Sex in Context* (Downs and Craft, 1997); *Let's Do It* (Scott *et al.*, 1997).

Stage 1: I can recognise some of my own feelings

The concepts are: sad, happy, angry, tired, pleasant/unpleasant; and the aims are to help pupils to understand and identify some of their feelings. There are cross-curriculum links to the English curriculum, Speaking and Listening.

☞ **Activity**

Working in a group, pupils are presented with a range of objects with different textures, and their responses to the feel of the textures on their skin are reflected by the teacher; e.g. 'You like the feel of the silk, don't you Peter?'. There are ideas for recognition of feelings in Let's Do It section 5. This activity can be extended by providing a variety of things to taste.

☞ **Activity**

Puppet work; using a simple design, get the pupils to make a happy and a sad puppet. Have them take it in turns to act something which makes them happy or sad, using their puppet.

Words used: sad/happy, nice/nasty.

Resources: materials with different textures such as fur, silk, hessian, cotton wool, etc.; foods for tasting such as marmalade, tomato sauce, lemon juice, soy sauce; *Let's Do It* (Scott *et al.*, 1994). Stick or plate puppets may be made from a stick with sellotape; faces are drawn on the plate to represent emotions, e.g. happy, sad.

Stage 5: I know how I feel (adolescence) and I can manage these feelings; I understand more complex feelings

The concepts are: puberty and change, feelings; and the aim is to identify some feelings which occur at puberty, including sexual feelings. There are cross-curriculum links to Body parts (module 1) stages 3 and 4 of this programme.

☞ **Activity**

Make a connection with the Body parts units on puberty, and discuss the way these changes can affect feelings, e.g. feeling moody.

☞ **Activity**

Section 3 of the video Piece by Piece looks at the personal skills necessary to deal with social situations. Watch this section of the video and discuss how the puppets Gary, Shelley and Pria feel and behave. Using the large cloth models (Brook – male and female models) pupils act out scenarios at the disco of youth club for meeting and feeling attracted to someone. This is a good way of exploring feelings. Let's Do It p119 describes an activity to learn about feelings in a sexual relationship and uses male and female models following a narrated story.

Words used: feeling, growing up, moods: sometimes I need..., sometimes I want...

Resources: video and notes *Piece by Piece* (Pavilion, 1996); *Let's Do It* (Scott *et al.*, 1997); *Picture My Feelings* (LDA, 1989); video and pack *My Choice, My Own Choice* (Clarke, 1992); puppet workshop *Baby Sam* (Gamlin, 1994).

Chapter 4

Family Life Education

This chapter introduces the concept of the family group and the idea that family groupings differ. While some children may live with a mother and father (mum and dad), others may live with either parent or grandparent, a stepmother or stepfather, relatives or guardians, or with carers in a residential setting.

Each person has his or her own role in the family. Some roles and relationships are constant, like being a daughter or a brother. Other roles can change as interests and circumstances change: a baby grows into a schoolchild, and may in time become the older brother or sister to another baby; a girl becomes a teenager; young people become more independent. Parents and carers can have different roles too. For instance, one may go out to work and the other stay with the children; both parents and carers may or may not go out to work, and all jobs at home may be done by either parent or carer.

Alongside an understanding of family styles and roles, pupils are encouraged to appreciate the importance of valuing themselves and others, and to know that everyone deserves respect. People have different gifts, and beginning to recognise their own strengths and those of their family and friends is an important step.

Within our school and community there is a diversity of cultures. It is important that pupils learn to respect this rich diversity and understand that families have their own way of leading their daily lives. The resource pack suggested in this chapter helps this understanding and so does the opportunity to explore attitudes through staff training. This acceptance permeates the whole school curriculum and is also studied specifically through religions in Religious Education, people and lifestyles in Geography, and literature in English.

More detailed aspects of family life and health are covered in Module 3, where pupils further their knowledge about child development and the responsibility of being a carer, and are given opportunities to acquire child care skills.

Figures 4.1 and 4.2 indicate how the work is presented at Piper Hill.

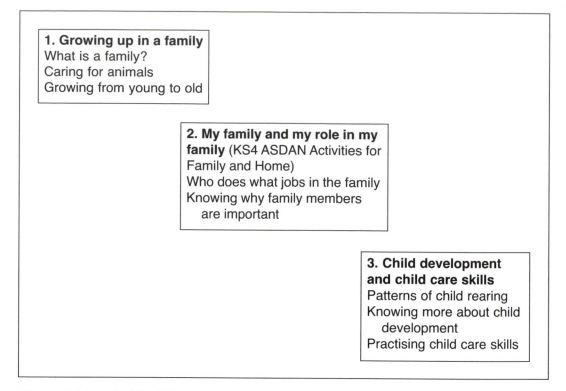

Figure 4.1 Family Life Education – the modules

Growing up in a family (module 1)

The teaching stages for the 'What is a Family?' part of the module are:
  ☐ I know what a family is and that there are different types of family.
  ☐ I know and respect the diversity in families.
  The following suggested activities help pupils first to explore their family and then to understand that there are lots of ways of being a family.

Stage 1: I know what a family is and that there are different types of family

The concept is: belonging, family. The aims are to recall memories and to heighten awareness of family members. There are cross-curricular links to RE – Belonging to a Family, and History.

☞ **Activity**
  In a comfortable atmosphere and in a small group, preferably one-to-one, introduce the Family Box (see Resources, p40). Keep using family names.

Term	Year	Curriculum	Class	N.C. Year
Spring	1998	PSE	Gp3	7

SOURCE:
Piper Hill PSE Curriculum
1. Family Life Education and Relationships
2. Relationships

AIMS:
- to understand that there are different types of families
- to understand roles in the family
- to value friendship
- to understand different relationships and how to behave

SPECIFIC TEACHING POINTS/OBJECTIVES:
- to understand that not all families are the same – parents, cultural background
- to understand that everyone is important
- to understand how we grow and change from baby to child to teenager to adulthood
- to talk about friends
- to talk about family
- to understand the importance of acceptable behaviour towards friends and family

ACTIVITIES/RESOURCES USED:
1. Draw pictures of own family
   'What is a family' game
   I am important because . . . my friend is important . . .
   Family statements – discuss. Are they true, false – why?
   Drama activities. Things I could do, can do, will be able to do.
2. Circle games: I am – I like . . . this is my friend . . . he likes . . . I like . . .
   because . . . Draw pictures, collages of friends and preferred activities (make puppets)
   Act out common scenes, e.g. falling out, playing, playground, talking to friends; different situations, meeting new friends

CROSS-CURRICULAR LINKS:
Drama
RE
English – writing

Figure 4.2 Family Life Education – sample of termly planning sheet

☞ **Activity**

Build up an album of pictures of family, extended family and favourite activities.

Words used: names of family members.

Resources: contents of Family Box, i.e. family photos, favourite possessions, something to remind the pupil of each family member (and pets), special smells (perhaps perfumes on lint in a tiny container), a tape of family voices, a tape of favourite songs or music heard at home, etc.

Stage 1: I know and respect the diversity in families

The concept is: family. The aim is to explore the diversity in families. There are cross-curricular links with RE and English Literature (e.g. *A Picture Book of Anne Frank'*, Adler, 1994; and *The Railway Children*, Nesbit, 1994)

☞ **Activity**

Working in pairs, pupils choose a photograph from the What is a Family? pack. They think of questions about the photograph; for example. 'what is the girl doing?', 'who is in this family?'. For those who find thinking of questions difficult, they could answer the teacher's questions.

☞ **Activity**

Divide the pupils into groups of three or four. Each group chooses a photograph from the What is a Family? pack, talks about it and acts out the scene on the photograph. If possible they develop this scene by acting out more of the scenes. Then they show their drama to the class who talk about the family in the drama.

Words used: family, mum, dad, sister, brother, grandad, grandma, baby, big, little, wedding, television, pushchair, breakfast, cat and dog, changing baby, bottle, wheelchair, house, homeless, play, birthday, meal, garden, Travellers.

Resources: *What is a Family?* (Development Education Centre, 1990), photographs and activities.

Some activities for the caring for animals part of the module are described below

Stage 2: I can care for young animals for a limited time, under supervision

The lesson plans and activities for this topic give the pupils an awareness that pets are not toys and that different pets have different needs:

☐ I know that young animals depend on their mothers (e.g. for food, to be washed, for protection – such as a kitten or a puppy).

☐ I know that they are very fragile and that I must be careful when looking after them (I can stroke them gently, pick them up gently, make a safe place for them to play so they do not hurt themselves, and keep dangerous objects out of their reach).

☐ I respect them and their right to be left alone if they want that (I recognise signs that tell me when they are happy and contented – dog wagging tail, cat purring – and learn that when I harass them they may bite or scratch me). And I make sure my pet has a quiet place to go to, if it wants.

☐ I know that young animals need food, water and clean bedding, and I can take some responsibility for some aspects of their care, e.g. they need food/drink regularly to grow.

☐ I learn that I can share my pet with others.

☐ I make sure my pets have exercise.

☐ I learn not to tease my pets.

☞ **Activity**

Invite a variety of pets into school and let the pupils name them and talk about them. Keep a record of any pets that pupils have at home.

☞ **Activity**

If possible, keep a school pet and encourage the children to take care of it. Keep a diary of the development, including photos.

☞ **Activity**

Organise visits to pet shops, aquariums, farms, zoos and any Pets Corner in your locality. Discuss the different habitats of the different animals that the children see, and the different foods they eat. How are the animals looked after?

☞ **Activity**

Invite a speaker from the RSPCA to talk about what the organisation does. Explore the roles of the RSPB and the Cat Protection League and discuss why there are animal shelters.

Growing from young to old

This is Stage 3 of Module 1 and the work is outlined in Figure 4.3. It will be seen that there are lots of cross-curricular links. Some suggestions for activities for this stage are listed below:

- A celebration of my birthday.
- A photo album of person from young to adult.
- A sequence of photos of young to old.
- Making booklets, e.g.'a baby can...', 'a child can...', 'a teenager can...', 'an adult can...', 'an old person can...'
- Lots of work on 'Stranger Danger' (see Chapter 5, module 1), e.g.visits from the police to discuss what to do if in danger; drama sessions – acting out scenarios; watching commercially produced videos.
- Individual road safety sessions; regular practice at crossing a road, identifying simple road signs.
- Making a simple journey to a local shop to buy ingredients for cookery.
- Regular cookery lessons to prepare own snack or simple meal.
- Preparing a class recipe book.
- Music: listening to pop music, making booklets about pop groups.
- Keeping teenage magazines in class – encouraging pupils to look at them and discuss fashion trends.
- Sharing magazines and discussing issues that are raised in them.

- Keeping newspaper clippings of important events and building up a diary of events over a year.
- Pupils keeping their own personal daily diary.
- Running a sandwich business in school: pupils preparing, collecting money and being paid each week from the proceeds of money collected.

Childhood
- ☐ Gender identification – where did I come from?
- ☐ I celebrate my birthday and those of my friends and family
- ☐ I can take on more responsibility for jobs around school and home
- ☐ The food I like to eat will change as I grow older e.g. baby food to adult food
- ☐ My body changes, e.g. I learn to walk, I have teeth to chew food as I get older
- ☐ I am becoming aware of different family members (e.g. grandma, who is old; baby sister, who is young)
- ☐ I am learning to be protective and helpful towards children and others who are less able or younger
- ☐ I moved to a different school when I was 11 years old
- ☐ I am becoming more sensitive to feelings and moods of others and can react accordingly

Teenager to Adult
- ☐ I am aware of my body changing, and that these changes are associated with puberty
- ☐ As I get older I am learning that I have different emotions (e.g. anger, fear, frustration, happiness, content)
- ☐ I know/experience teenage music, and I am familiar with pop groups
- ☐ I explore teenage fashions (e.g. The Clothes Show)
- ☐ I may have links with a local college
- ☐ I may go on work experience
- ☐ I may be paid for work that I do
- ☐ I may go to discos
- ☐ I may have more freedom to go out by myself
- ☐ I may have friendships outside the home (e.g. youth club)
- ☐ I may be using public transport
- ☐ I may be going shopping for simple articles
- ☐ I may be dealing with my emotions
- ☐ I am learning to identify differences between friendships and boy friend/girl friend relationships
- ☐ I make deliberate decisions about what I like/don't like

Figure 4.3 Exploring the human life cycle – the stages

Adult
- ☐ I am aware of adults in my world
- ☐ I am aware that some adults become mothers and fathers
- ☐ I am aware that some adults go to work every day
- ☐ I am aware that adults may marry
- ☐ I am aware that I can make some decisions for myself, and my decision should be respected (e.g. the clothes I wear, what TV programmes I can watch, what time I can stay up to)
- ☐ I might not live at home: I might live with a group of other adults in a group home
- ☐ I am aware that adults do different jobs (e.g. people in the community who help us, such as doctor, nurse, policeman/woman)
- ☐ I am aware of the role of intimate relationships
- ☐ I recognise factors involved in setting up a home, and in planning parenthood

Adult to Old Person
- ☐ I am aware that one day I will grow old
- ☐ I can name some factors that might occur (e.g. my hair may go grey, I may have wrinkles on my face, my body will slow down)
- ☐ I know about grandparents and their place in the family
- ☐ I am aware that when I am old, I may have health problems (e.g. I may need hearing aids, a walking stick, special medicines)
- ☐ I am aware that some people when they are old may live in a nursing home
- ☐ I am aware that very old people need to be looked after
- ☐ I know that some old people are very lonely

Death
- ☐ I know that some people become ill
- ☐ I know that sometimes illness cannot be made better
- ☐ I know that we all die

Figure 4.3 continued

My family and my role in my family (module 2)

At Piper Hill, we use ASDAN Transition Challenge KS4:PSE – Family/Home for much of the work in this module (see Figure 4.4 and Figure 11.3, p104). The teaching stages are shown in Figure 4.5. See Chapter 11 for more information about ASDAN.

Stage 1: I know who does which job in my family; and I know how I can help

The concepts are: helping in the family, a job. The aim is to complete the ASDAN activity Family/Home – Independent Living Skills, KS4. There are cross-curricular links to English – Speaking and Listening.

☞ **Activity**
  Pupils bring photos of their family from home and the names of their family members. These photos are all put together on a wall display which can also include staff family photographs.

☞ Activity

Using photographs or pictures of household and gardening jobs such as cooking, cleaning the car and so on, pupils name the tasks and then say who does which of these jobs in their family. They can record this in chart form, as the example below.

Who does these jobs in your home?					
(Substitute the names of family members for column headings in pupil's individual chart)	Adult male	Adult female	Male child	Female child	Other
Washing up					
Cooking					
Cleaning					
Household repairs					
Gardening					
Changing plugs					
Washing clothes					
Paying bills					
Decorating					
Ironing					
Making beds					
Food shopping					

Year 1 – Autumn Term	Spring Term	Summer Term
Family/Home – Independent Living Skills	**Family/Home – Self-Advocacy**	**Family/Home – Personal Autonomy**
Show you know who does what jobs in your family. Suggest three ways to help.	Say why different family members are important to you. Choose appropriate birthday presents for them.	Show you know how to ask for help when you need it. Show how to let others know when you don't need help.
Year 2 – Autumn Term	**Spring Term**	**Summer Term**
Family/Home and Science – Positive Self-Image	**Family/Home – Personal Development**	**Family/Home**
Open activity which you and your family/carer can choose. Take part in personal hygiene activities. Show you know the names of different body parts. Understand that it can be inappropriate to touch or be touched in particular places.	Choose a daily routine with your family. Show you understand what you have to do and when.	In the sixth term the pupils' work is assembled for final accreditation.

Figure 4.4 ASDAN Transition Challenge KS4 – PSE

ASDAN – TRANSITION CHALLENGE	
Name:	Family/Home: Independent Living Skills and Self-Advocacy

ACTIVITY

1. Show you know who does what jobs in your family. Suggest three ways in which you might be able to help.
2. Use photographs or pictures to say why different members of your family are important to you. Choose an appropriate present you might buy for each person's birthday.

• I can name my family members
 	
• I can name jobs which are done in a family (in mine and in others)
 	
• I can say who does what jobs in my family
 	
• I can say three ways in which I could help:
 	
   1.
 	
   2.
 	
   3.
 	
• I can say what family members mean to me and I know why they are important
 	
• I can match pictures of gifts to my family members	

EVIDENCE

Form:

Trans.Chall.Ind.Living Skills

Figure 4.5 ASDAN record sheet, showing the teaching stages

Words used: job, family, help, cook, clean, wash clothes, tidy up, wash up, iron, mow lawn, make beds, shopping, mend things.

Resources: photographs from home, photographs or pictures of people doing household jobs, ASDAN Award pupil record book published as part of the scheme.

Stage 2: I can say what family members mean to me and I know why they are important; I can choose a gift for each of my family members

The concepts are: importance of family members, birthdays and gifts. The aims are to complete ASDAN activity Family/Home self-Advocacy. There are cross-curricular links to English – Speaking and Listening.

☞ **Activity**
Pupils look at a photo of their family members and talk about each person who helps or is special to them. They could discuss which activities they like to share together.

☞ **Activity**
Pupils look in a variety of catalogues and cut out pictures of appropriate presents for their family. This can be extended by pupils visiting the shops and picking out items which may be suitable gifts for their family members.

Words used: important, help, care, to like, birthday, gift, give, choose.

Resources: family photographs for each pupil; catalogues to choose gifts.

Child development and child care skills (module 3)

By now, pupils are aware that there are different customs, traditions and ways of approaching everyday living. This patterns of child rearing stage of the module develops awareness. For example:

- There are different ways of feeding babies: breast-feeding, bottle-feeding, weaning.
- There are different ways of carrying babies: wrapped in a shawl, papoose style, in a buggy, in a pram.
- There are different sleep patterns: family rituals at bedtime differ.
- There are different discipline patterns.
- There are variations in mealtime patterns: family meals, TV meals, adults and children eating separately.
- Family care can be extended beyond the immediate parents, guardians or carers: to grandparents, aunts, uncles, friends, neighbours, older members of the extended family such as step sisters or step brothers.
- Child rearing differs both within different communities in this country and abroad: the Kibbutz system in Israel; the one child per family system in China; in some countries large families are actively encouraged.

Stage 2: I understand that there are different patterns of child rearing

The concepts are: care/security, acceptance, difference/same. The aims are to emphasise diversity, and to affirm the pattern of care within each child's experience.

There are cross-curricular links with the study of religions and cultures in RE, lifestyles in Geography, and through our Equal Opportunities policies.

☞ **Activity**

On the theme 'who cares for you', build up a personal book/chart of everyone involved in the care of a pupil. Photographs, reminders, comments. These can be looked at, compared, celebrated.

☞ **Activity**

(This is a cross-curricular activity with Geography.) Over several lessons, look at being a child: around the world. Use artefacts, dress, pictures, books and video. Create a 'world' frieze of children. Make comparisons with being a child in your own school.

Words used: family words: mother, father, aunt, uncle, etc.; also special names; cultural words, i.e. for clothing, rituals, family, home, countries; love, care, different/same, home, family, custom, way.

Resources: cultural clothing and artefacts; story books about family life; pictures of a variety of families/groupings; videos of a family life around the world; personal photographs; visitors.

I know in more detail about child development

- ☐ I know the importance of talking and playing with babies and young children
- ☐ I know that smiling, crying, babbling and experimenting with sounds are about learning to communicate
- ☐ I know that babies and toddlers wear nappies and need changing regularly until they are toilet trained
- ☐ I know that babies drink milk from the breast or a bottle, and are weaned onto food between three and six months
- ☐ I know that a baby's teeth grow slowly, a toddler should have a full set of milk teeth by 18 months
- ☐ I know that toddlers will want to feed themselves with a spoon, and will be able to chew their food
- ☐ I know that most babies will learn to crawl, pull themselves up and will walk before they are 18 months old

I know about the role of primary health care

- ☐ I understand the roles of the doctor, district nurse, health visitor, dentist and optician within the local community
- ☐ I know the role of the local hospital: that there are outpatients and casualty departments as well as wards where people go for medical treatment
- ☐ I know that I may be taken to the doctor if I am unwell
- ☐ I know that I should have my teeth examined regularly by the dentist
- ☐ I know that babies should be taken to the clinic regularly to be weighed, and to check that they are developing well
- ☐ I know that there are regular medical, dental and auditory checks for primary school children
- ☐ I know that a variety of medical information, advice, leaflets etc. are available at the local clinic, health centre or doctor's surgery

---

Figure 4.6 Module 3, Stages 3 and 4, in more detail

I know that vaccination and immunisation help to prevent disease

☐ I know there is a programme of vaccination and immunisation for babies, a booster programme when children are five years old and before young people leave school

☐ I know that extra protection may also be needed when travelling abroad

☐ I know that information is available from clinics, health centres, doctor's surgeries and school

---

I know and understand about putting into practice the skills of child care

☐ I know that young children need clean air to breath, plenty of light and warmth, a good balanced diet (and to learn to feed themselves)

☐ I know that young children need a clean environment and the facility to be clean and to learn how to keep clean, and the facility to learn to use the toilet

☐ I know that young children need to have freedom to move and play in safety

☐ I know that young children need to have regular patterns in daily life, including regular meals and a regular sleep pattern

☐ I am aware of safety issues connected with handling, feeding and playing with young children.

☐ I understand about potential hazards in the home and outside

---

I know about helping agencies which support families and individuals in different circumstances

☐ I know about statutory services such as: social services, home from home care, respite care, local police service, hospital transport/taxi, day care: nurseries, children's centres, health teams: physiotherapist, speech and language therapist

☐ I know about voluntary and grant aided services such as: playgroups/toddlers' groups, after school clubs, play and holiday schemes, junior/senior youth clubs, community centre activities, MENCAP, Catholic Rescue Society, Childline, Dr Barnardo's, whole family support, Families in Crisis, Relate, Faith community groups: e.g., Sunday school, Rainbow Trust/hospice movement

---

Figure 4.6 continued

In the second part of module 3 pupils learn about child development in more detail and in the third part practise child care skills; the learning stages are summarised in Figure 4.6. Preliminary work on Childhood has been done in Module 1 (see Figure 4.3) and Life Cycles is one of the modules in the Sex Education programme (Chapter 3).

Stage 3: I know in more detail about child development

The concepts are: change, growth, play, dependence. The aim is to teach the concept of growth from babyhood to childhood, awareness of the physical changes, and that babies and children are dependent on adults for care. There are cross-curricular links with Science.

☞ **Activity**

Over a term, arrange visits to the class by a baby and a toddler (children of staff or parents). Compare growth and change between visits and between children, e.g. take photographs, tape the noises the children made. Encourage pupils to help with some care tasks, e.g. feeding, bathing, changing a nappy and play.

☞ **Activity**

Prepare for pupils to spend up to three lessons in a toddler group or day nursery, getting to know and playing with the children. Preparation: look at toys suitable for babies and toddlers.

☞ **Activity**

Organise the preparation of a meal for a baby, a toddler and a three year old.

Words used: growing, changing, baby, toddler, child, boy/male, girl/female, care, play, toy, crawl, walk, run, feeding, breast, bottle, nappy – various types.

Resources: friendly toddler group, nursery, babies, toddlers known to class; books about babies and children – both story and resource books, pictures and videos; build up resource boxes – things for a baby/things for a toddler.

Stage 3: I know about the role of primary health care

The concepts are: health care for everyone; personal responsibility for health care; feelings – well and not well.

The aim is that pupils are aware of the different people who can care for them medically. There are cross-curricular links to Personal History.

☞ **Activity**

Have the children make a diary of their own dental/ophthalmic and doctor or hospital visits, and injections received, with pictures, drawings and explanations. Make a similar diary for a new born baby over a year, linked to a practical study.

☞ **Activity**

Organise group visits for all the pupils (to include sensory experiences) to dentist, optician and health centre, Health Education Department (hospital) and chemist.

Words used: clinic, doctor, ill, poorly, temperature, sore, hurt, nurse, health visitor, optician, audiologist, injection, medication, safe.

Resources: diaries/notebooks for pupils.

Stage 4: I know about helping agencies which support families and individuals in different circumstances

The concepts are: support, need, asking for help, discussion. The aims are that pupils understand that there are many agencies, and that it is okay to ask for help; and that there are people who run clubs, playgroups and the like voluntarily. There are cross-curricular links with RE (groups within Faith communities), History (origins of agencies such as Dr Barnardo's).

☞ **Activity**

Organise some visits to clubs, centres, playgroups or similar and arrange some visits from group organisers, leaders, workers, so that they can talk to the class about their work and the services provided by their organisation. Use pictures, video, books/pamphlets to explore concepts through discussion and role play.

Words used: club, centre, playscheme, family, care, help, clinic, health centre, nursery, playgroup, specific agency words.

Resources: agency people, books, pamphlets, pictures, videos.

Chapter 5

Personal Safety

Helping pupils to keep safe is an important part of the PSE curriculum and is an area which parents and carers generally are keen should be covered in school.

Teaching Personal Safety as a topic raises some issues. For instance, pupils need to learn the meaning of the word 'stranger', and to be taught strategies for keeping safe without becoming too fearful. In the examples of lessons which follow, pupils learn to practise how to protect themselves in the safety of a supportive group, through stories, games and role play.

It is important to teach pupils to recognise when they do not feel safe and which adults they can ask for help, depending on the situation. Teaching about safety always involves developing pupils' self-esteem, confidence and ability to make choices. One of the best ways of doing this is through group building activities.

The Police/School Liaison Officer can play an important role in working with teachers on safety issues and forging valuable links between the school and the wider community. The examples of activities for stranger danger and road safety given here were developed at Piper Hill through working with our Police School Liaison Officer.

Group building activities

The following group building activities are suitable for building up self-esteem in preparation for personal safety modules (this section is based on *Protection Pack*, LDA, 1994):

- The 'All Change' game: leader calls out a category and everyone in that category changes places (e.g. everyone with long hair). Pupils take turns to be leader.
- Say something positive about someone without mentioning their name and others have to guess who it is. Take turns being leader.
- Gender-sorting clothes, both outer- and underwear.
- Guessing what an object is under a cloth. Questions can be asked of the leader, who can only say 'yes' or 'no'.
- Pupils look at magazines in pairs, finding categories of people – e.g. male/female, children, etc.
- Pupils look at magazines and find pictures of people who are happy. Ask what makes group members happy.

- Play Kim's Game with a tray of clothing/wash bag items. Name the items and discuss them. Then cover the tray with a cloth and remove an item without the class seeing it. Uncover the tray: pupils have to say which item is missing.
- Body movement activity: go round the group: each person has to do something and the rest can copy – e.g. nod, wink, wave, clap, stand up.
- A 'leader says' game – e.g. Linda says 'stand up'. Those who don't follow instructions are 'out'. Pupils take turns to be leader.

Stranger danger (module 1)

The teaching stages for this module are:
☐ I am learning about keeping myself-safe at school, in the community, and in the locality.
☐ I understand 'yes' and 'no', and using these words according to how I feel.
☐ I understand the concept of 'stranger'.
☐ I am developing confidence to deal with a threatening situation.
☐ I can practise getting out of a dangerous situation.
☐ I am learning how, when and who to ask for help.

Stage 1: I am learning about keeping myself-safe (stranger danger – the car)

The concepts are: awareness of strangers, 'yes' and 'no' skills, asking/giving permission skills, assertion skills. The aim is to develop understanding and awareness of the dangers of 'strangers' in different settings.

☞ **Activity**
Yes/no games: The teacher introduces a tray of objects (such as a pen, a mug, a comb, a book), and makes sure each pupil knows the objects by asking them to identify them correctly and point out each in turn. Then the teacher holds up an object and pupils must answer yes or no to the question whether it is the item named. When pupils can answer yes or no correctly, move to the next stage, Kim's Game. Allow the pupils time to memorise the same set of objects on the tray, then cover them and secretly remove one item. The pupils have then to say what is missing; for instance, the teacher asks 'is the mug missing?' and they answer yes or no. Next, to develop pupils' ability to answer 'no', the teacher presents them with a choice of experiences. Ask them, for instance, if they want to wear a silly hat, be sprayed with water, or put paint on their hands; affirm them when they say no (no, of course you don't), thus encouraging them that it is okay to say no.

☞ **Activity**
What is a stranger?: The teacher invites a trusted colleague who is unknown to the pupils to come to the classroom or school grounds during a lesson and ask the pupils to go somewhere with him/her. At this point the teacher intervenes and reinforces the message not to go with strangers. Follow this with a class discussion about the meaning of 'stranger'.

☞ **Activity**

Begin with a group building activity: for example, the teacher passes around objects starting with a large object such as a big ball, gradually getting smaller down to the size of a grain of rice. Present a story of a girl going home and a man inviting her to get into a car (e.g. The Car from the LDA Protection Pack). Discuss the story: What is the right thing to do? Follow up with practical drama: use a parked car in the car park belonging to a member of staff and let the pupils take it in turns to act out the story.

Words used: yes, no, safe, stranger, dangerous, friend.

Resources: tray of variously sized objects and cloth; *Protection Pack* (LDA, 1994).

Stage 1: I am learning about keeping myself-safe (stranger danger – at football)

The concepts are: awareness of strangers, listening to others, assertion, voicing of opinions, confidence-building. The aim is to develop understanding and awareness of the dangers of 'strangers' in all kinds of settings.

☞ **Activity**

Start with a group building activity – get pupils to look through magazines or catalogues in pairs for items of clothing that would suit each other. Present a story of a man asking a boy playing football to come with him (e.g. Paul Plays Football from the LDA Protection Pack). Follow up with a drama activity where the pupils act out the scene in the book, especially reinforcing the parts where Paul tells the man to go away and where he tells his teacher.

☞ **Activity**

Group building. Have the pupils working with a partner giving and accepting compliments, being positive, then feed these positive statements back to the group.

☞ **Activity**

In a group, practise saying 'go away!' in a whisper, then getting louder and louder. A pupil is chosen as leader to 'conduct' the group chant and tell them when to stop.

Words used: yes, no, l like, I don't like, help!, go away.

Resources: magazines or catalogues; *Protection Pack* (LDA, 1994).

Stage 1: I am learning about keeping myself-safe (stranger danger – taking photographs)

The concepts here are: permission, decision making, assertion, negotiation; and the aim is to encourage self-advocacy, i.e. that pupils are aware that no one should take a photograph of them if they don't wish it.

☞ **Activity**

Introduce a bag of mixed clothing items and encourage comments and discussion, in particular whether it is appropriate to show them in a private or public place, according to where on your body you wear them. Tell or read a story of a girl sunbathing and a man taking photographs of her (e.g. The Photograph from the Protection Pack.) Talk about the story. Let the pupils take photographs of one another, encouraging those who want to say 'no'.

☞ **Activity**
Start with a group building activity identifying gender through clothes – talk about what is appropriate to wear for each gender. Pupils dress up if they want to, and choose whether to say yes or no to being photographed.

Words used: yes, no, safe, public, private.
Resources: a bag of clothes, including underwear; camera; *Protection Pack* (LDA, 1994).

Getting help (module 2)

The teacher stages for this module are:
- ☐ I know who can help me at home, school and in the community (parents/carers, teachers, friends, police, nurse etc.).
- ☐ I know how to ask for help from a safe adult (this is part of the ASDAN Family/Home Personal Autonomy activity, see Chapter 10, Advocacy).
- ☐ I know my name and address.
- ☐ I can use the telephone.
- ☐ I can call the emergency services if needed.

Stage 1: I know my name and address and can use the telephone to call the emergency services

The concept is: use of emergency services. The aims are that pupils should be able to call the police/fire if help were needed, that they should be able to remember their home address and are capable of explaining an incident over the phone and relaying essential information. There are cross-curricular links to English – Speaking and Listening.

☞ **Activity**
Arrange a visit for a police officer to talk about how and when to phone the police. Get the pupils to act out making a telephone call and try to get them to say their own name and address clearly. If possible make use of a video recorder, so that there can be playback and discussion.

☞ **Activity**
Arrange a visit from an ambulance person to talk about the job. Practise making a telephone call to this emergency service, trying to ensure pupils say their own name and address clearly. Video if possible. Looking at the replay of the video give some hints about how each person could improve.

Words used: 999, Help!, pupils' own addresses.
Resources: video camera, TV, visits from a Police School Liaison Officer and ambulance personnel.

Living with traffic (module 3)

The teaching stages for this module are:
- ☐ I understand the dangers of roads and the importance of walking safely.
- ☐ I understand about safe clothing (being seen in bright clothing, wearing safe footwear, and why cyclists wear headgear).

☐ I know the importance of looking and listening in relation to traffic.
☐ I know the rule for crossing the road: stop, look, listen and think.
☐ I can practise crossing the road at safe places.
☐ I can use public transport with an adult.
☐ I can make a journey independently, using public transport.
☐ I understand where it is safe to play.

Stage 1: I know the importance of looking and listening in relation to traffic

The concepts are: developing listening skills; understanding that it is harder to hear with a hat or hood on, ears covered up. The aim is to develop looking and listening skills in relation to traffic. There are cross-curricular links to Science.

☞ **Activity**

Ask the pupils to close their eyes and listen carefully. Then have them make a list of sounds heard (e.g. talking in the next room, footsteps in the corridor, birds singing outside). Practise the recognition of other sounds and the direction they come from in the classroom (e.g. closing a drawer, dropping a pencil). Do the exercises once more, then repeat them with the children wearing hoods. What difference does it make?

☞ **Activity**

Take the pupils for a walk outside. Practise with them identifying traffic sounds (far and near). Back in the classroom, play a game of traffic-sounds lotto.

Words used: safe, loud, quiet, far, near.
Resources: bells, keys, instruments, hats, hoods, traffic sounds lotto.

Stage 1: I understand where it is safe to play

The concepts are: 'awareness of danger while playing, dangers of the road'. The aims are to raise pupils' awareness of where to play safely in their own environment, and to raise awareness of the dangers of the road. There are cross-curricular links to Science.

☞ **Activity**

Introduce a variety of indoor and outdoor toys and start a discussion about playing with them. Where do you play? Is it safe? Show photographs to help the discussion along. Take the group to the park and talk to the pupils about its safety aspect. Emphasise adult supervision.

☞ **Activity**

Help the pupils to record scenes on video acted by themselves which demonstrate awareness of dangers – e.g. do not play near parked cars (staff car park), safe crossing of a road, playing safely. Pupils should then watch their own video and discuss.

Words used: safe, dangerous, garden, playground/parks, road, pavement, kerb, stop/go, stop, look, listen.
Resources: pictures or photos of gardens and parks, indoor/outdoor toys, camcorder and video tape.

Chapter 6

Health Related Exercise

Cross-curricular links

Health Related Exercise is taught mainly through our Physical Education curriculum. There are also links with the Food and Nutrition (Food Technology) curriculum in modules 2 and 10 on Healthy Eating. At Piper Hill, we also have a lunchtime club (the Body Beautiful Club, described in Chapter 10, p99), set up with the pupils, which encourages exercise and healthy eating.

In addition, the theme of keeping healthy through exercise runs through the general school curriculum, and activities to work towards this are built into the daily routine. There are many ways in which this can be done, for example you can select specific times when regular exercise takes place during the school day, such as PE, dance, swimming, hydro, outdoor playtimes, games (indoor and outdoor). Allocate time before and after the exercise for discussion.

1. Key concepts or ideas before exercise could include food (what the pupils have eaten for breakfast/lunch/snack: stress the importance of this to give us energy which we will need for the activity to come). This could lead to work on healthy foods for some groups.
2. Review with the pupils what they have been doing that day so far: working/sitting/thinking. Lead this round to the idea that it would now be good to move, run, jump, get some fresh air, and so on. You can discuss what activities they enjoy and perhaps give an element of choice. Key concepts after exercise could include food and drink (do they feel hungry or thirsty? we need food/drink to give us energy).
3. After exercise, when pupils have used up all their energy, they need to sit and rest for a bit. Discuss their likes and dislikes – did they enjoy the exercise and how do they feel? Do they feel good and would they like to do it again?
4. For pupils with PMLD, responses to different exercises and physical activities can be recorded to note their likes, dislikes and preferences, to work towards choice making.

One specific module is described in the following section, which aims to teach that food gives us energy, and that regular exercise makes us feel better and helps us to grow strong and have a fit and healthy body.

Fitness and health (module 1)

The teaching stages for this module are:
- ☐ I know that I feel better when I take regular exercise.
- ☐ I know that exercise uses energy which comes from food.
- ☐ I know that it is important to exercise regularly to have a fit and healthy body.

Stage 1: know that exercise uses energy which comes from food

The concept is: the links between food, energy and exercise. The aims are that pupils can name or point or sign the names of common foods, and that they taste variety and state preferences, and choices. There are cross-curricular links to Sensory Science, Food Technology, English, Maths.

☞ **Activity**

Organise a Lucky Dip: put some real food items in bags or boxes (one type per week). The pupils take turns to pick and label or sign what they are. Use pictures of breakfast foods or lunch foods for a daily group activity. Each pupil is to say or point to their breakfast/lunch and Blu-tack its name next to it.

☞ **Activity**

Have a tasting session related to the food items of the week; record responses to look for preferences and choice making, likes/dislikes, more/no more etc.

Words used: food names, good/bad, like/don't like, thirsty and hungry, after, finished.
Resources: bags of food, pictures and photos.

Stage 1: know that exercise uses energy which comes from food.

The concept is: the links between food, energy and exercise. The aim is that pupils understand that energy comes from food and exercise uses energy. There are cross-curricular links with PE and Food and Nutrition.

☞ **Activity**

Before a sports activity, let the pupils talk about how they feel; that is, they have energy and are ready for activity. After completing their activity, pupils talk about how they feel; that is, they are tired, they need to rest and drink to replace fluids and to eat to get back more energy.

☞ **Activity**

Pupils look at photos of athletes and talk about the activities they do or are doing and how they get their energy to perform. Look at a variety of low and high energy foods and decide which ones athletes need to eat for energy.

Words used: names of food types, exercise, energy, use up/get, tired, thirsty, fluids/drinks, names of sports and sporting activities.
Resources: pictures of photos of athletes; examples of high energy foods such as bananas, pasta and chocolate, and low energy foods as apples, thin soups and a cup of tea.

Chapter 7

Food and Nutrition

At Piper Hill, Food and Nutrition was originally developed and taught as part of our Personal and Social Education curriculum. This was changed to follow National Curriculum guidelines so that pupils could study Food Technology as part of Food and Nutrition, thus expanding our earlier curriculum. Since 1997, Food and Nutrition has been developed at INSET teachers' meetings and consequently rewritten by the Food Technology coordinator. The subject is now timetabled and taught by designated staff as part of our Food Technology curriculum. Two of our staff have attended a Food Hygiene and Handling course.

This chapter includes the relevant sections of our Food Technology curriculum (see Figure 7.1) which are also part of Food and Nutrition for Personal and Social Education. Pupils in our FE department also run a sandwich business as part of a Careers curriculum. (This is not described in this book.)

Food Technology		
Each Module to be taught for half a term (6/7 weeks)		
K S 3	Y 7 Introduction to Food Technology Room	Healthy eating Module 2
	Y 8 Safety in the kitchen Module 3	Planning and making a simple meal Module 4
	Y 9 What's on a label	Breakfast foods Module 6
K S 4	Y 10 Weights and measures	Food groups (Vitamins) Module 8
	Y 11 Packaging and ingredients	Healthy eating Module 10
F E	Y 12 – Food, Glorious Food – Careers	
	Y 12 –Y14 – Sandwich business ——————————————————→	

Figure 7.1 The Food Technology curriculum; modules 2, 3, 4, 6, 8 and 10 relate to Food and Nutrition

Food Technology at Piper Hill

Food Technology aims to develop pupils' knowledge of the constituents of a nutritionally balanced and healthy diet and to develop the skills needed to prepare food whilst being aware of the relevant Health and Safety issues. Through developing these skills and knowledge the majority of pupils are enabled to become as independent as possible when leaving school. For some pupils Food Technology is of a more experiential nature, focusing on the sensory aspects of food, but the same module titles are used across all the teaching groups.

Issues and attitudes

There are important issues to bear in mind. Medical conditions need to be carefully documented and diets observed, for example allergies to food substances and diabetic diets. Religious and cultural issues should be considered when planning work, for example observation of the Halal diet for Muslim pupils..

We recommend that schools work closely with staff on defining important issues and on exploring attitudes to food when developing their Food and Nutrition curriculum. At the end of this chapter – after the module descriptions and activities – there are details of the workshop Attitudes to Food (Figure 7.9) which we ran for staff at Piper Hill School, together with accompanying notes.

Hygiene and safety rules

Health and Safety is crucially important and is an integral part of all Food and Nutrition work (see Figure 7.2) Text in this section is largely taken from *Working with Food in Primary Schools* – ISBN 095216454X – (Ridgewell, 1997). This book is available from Ridgewell Press, PO Box 3425, London SW19 4AP.

What to wear for food work

All people working with food should wear special clothes to protect the food from being contaminated. In Piper Hill we keep aprons just for food work, which are kept separate. Everyone should observe the same hygiene standards, so teachers, helpers and pupils should all wear protective clothing during food work.

Preparing foods

During food preparation pupils should learn the importance of personal hygiene and food-handling. Have notices displayed in appropriate places reminding pupils of items on the following check-list.

- Avoid preparing food if you feel sick, have diarrhoea, colds with runny noses and coughs, or other infections.
- Cover all cuts with a clean, waterproof dressing – you can use blue coloured plasters for food work which show up if they drop into food.
- Always wash hands after using the toilet and before food work.
- Tie back long hair before starting food work – keep a box of elastic bands for the purpose.

The Acts

Health and Safety at Work Act 1974

This Act applies to schools and it protects teachers and pupils from risks to health and safety arising out of their need to work. Schools need codes of practice for safe working and first aid.

Food Safety Act 1990

The Food Safety Act 1990 came into force in January 1991 to replace the Food Act 1984. The Food Safety Act was introduced to take into account changes in food technology and eating habits. It was designed to help reduce the number of cases of food-borne illness such as food poisoning and contamination. The Food Safety Act covers the whole of the food chain from the farm to the food shop and refers to the sale of all food. Food premises must be registered and anyone preparing food for sale must be registered and come under the control of the Act. The Act applies to food businesses in England, Scotland and Wales. In Northern Ireland the Food Safety (Northern Ireland) Order 1991 applies.

Food Safety (General Food Hygiene) Regulations 1995

These regulations lay down the rules of hygiene and require food businesses to assess the risks in making their food products and take any required action to ensure the safety of the food. Hazard Analysis and Critical Control Points (HACCP) is an example of a system that ensures controls are appropriate.

Food Safety (Temperature Control) Regulations 1995

These regulations state that the catering industry must meet certain temperature requirements for food storage, cooking and reheating. A maximum chill temperature of 8°C is a specific requirement, subject to certain exemptions, for foods that pose a potential microbiological hazard.

Cooked or reheated food that needs to be kept hot must be kept at a temperature at or above 63°C.

Control of Substances Hazardous to Health Regulations 1994 (COSSH)

These regulations provide a framework for the control of hazardous substances in all types of businesses including food businesses. The regulations require risk assessments to be carried out before certain substances can be used in schools. Hazardous substances must be avoided in the classroom. Hazardous substances can be found in cleaners' cupboards, and teachers can make harmful substances during work with micro-organisms, such as letting food decay, and chemical experiments.

Figure 7.2 Health and Safety: the law and official advice

- Wear clean, protective aprons or overalls during food preparation.
- Remove jewellery before food work – you need a safe storage space.
- Roll or tie up sleeves before you start.
- When ready to begin, wash your hands well.
- Never sneeze or cough over food.
- Always wash hands after handling raw and uncooked foods.
- Do not touch your face, hair or other parts of your body when working with food.

Keeping food cool

In school it is important to keep perishable food cool at temperatures at or below 5°C in a refrigerator. The aim of using a refrigerator is to keep things cool. The refrigerator must not only operate effectively, but food needs to be properly packed and stored within the cabinet. Care should be taken not to leave the door open to let in warm air. Observe the following refrigerator rules:

- Keep the refrigerator clean and operating at 5°C or below.
- Keep all food covered using a plate or cling film.
- Store raw and cooked food separately.
- Don't overpack the refrigerator.
- Don't leave the door open for too long.
- Let hot food cool before putting in the refrigerator – the cooling time for hot food should not exceed 90 minutes.
- Cover raw meat and poultry and store on a shelf below cooked food.
- Use a refrigerator thermometer to check that the temperature is maintained at 5°C or below – pupils can keep a weekly record for good practice.
- Do not allow any food to drip onto foods below.

Making food hot

Follow these guidelines when heating food:
- Be aware of fire regulations when heating food.
- Cookers, hotplates and multi-cookers should only be used with supervision.
- The whole class should know about the dangers of hot things during practical activities.
- Place a suitable work-surface next to cookers on which to stand hot dishes.
- Never leave hot tins, saucepans or cookers unattended.
- Always carry hot dishes with thick oven gloves which are in good repair.

To make sure food is safe to eat, all food, however it is cooked, must be piping hot right through. High temperatures and a long enough time will destroy bacteria. This means the food should reach a temperature of at least 72°C for two minutes. This temperature can be measured using a food probe.

When heating food in the microwave cooker, stir, turnover, rearrange the food or turn the container frequently so that the microwave can penetrate the food evenly. Foods should be heated until they reach 72°C for two minutes at the coldest point. Test using a temperature probe which has been disinfected with a special antibacterial wipe. Food cooked in the microwave cooker should have standing time so that the heat can flow through to the centre of the food to give an even temperature distribution.

Healthy eating (module 2)

Pupilss will begin to recognise that some foods are good for us and that some foods are not so good for us. The 'traffic light' system will be introduced – red and green category foods. The foods will be sorted into different categories. Pupilss will have the opportunity to look at packaging for healthy symbols. They will have the opportunity to make healthy snacks. Hygiene and safety rules will be followed.

The teaching stages are listed on the Certificate of Achievement for this module (see Figure 7.3).

Food Technology
Certificate of Achievement

Module Number 2
Healthy Eating

In successfully completing this module

....

has demonstrated that he/she

1. can sort some foods into healthy and not so healthy categories, e.g.:

2. can follow simple hygiene rules, e.g.:

3. can follow simple safety rules, e.g.:

4. can identify the healthy eating symbol on packaging, e.g.:

5. can participate in making a healthy snack, e.g.:

6. can use some of the specified key skills, e.g.: (please tick)

    spreading ☐   cutting ☐
    opening ☐   washing ☐

Figure 7.3 Certificate of Achievement showing teaching stages for Module 2

Safety in the kitchen (module 3)

The purpose of this module is to develop safety skills when working in the kitchen. The pupils will work on using heat safely, using knives safely and rules on using electricity safely. Pupils will have the opportunity to use a kettle and use a hob, and will be taught general kitchen first aid. Activities will focus around food/drinks that require heat and the use of pans.

The teaching stages are listed on the Certificate of Achievement for this module (see Figure 7.4).

Food Technology
Certificate of Achievement

Module Number 3
Safety in the Kitchen

In successfully completing this module

....

has demonstrated that he/she

1. can use the power switches appropriately, e.g.:

2. can use a kettle appropriately

3. can show awareness of the danger of hot water

4. can show awareness of the dangers of heat

5. can show awareness of first aid in the kitchen

6. can show awareness of the danger of sharp knives

7. can recall some of the main elements of the safety video

8. can recall and explain some of the key words: (please tick)

hot	☐	sharp	☐	hob	☐
dangerous	☐	cut	☐	kettle	☐
cold	☐	steam	☐		

Figure 7.4 Certificate of Achievement showing teaching stages for Module 3

Planning and making a simple meal (module 4)

This module will help students develop the organisational skills necessary to the task of making a simple meal. The pupils will develop their knowledge of the geography of the kitchen and continue to develop safety and hygiene skills. Pupils will be encouraged to make a realistic meal choice. They will make a shopping list and shop for a meal. The task will include taking out the correct equipment and awareness of the time limit to complete the task. The pupils will set the table and invite a friend to share the meal.

The teaching stages are listed on the Certificate of Achievement for this module (see Figure 7.5).

Food Technology
Certificate of Achievement

Module Number 4
Planning and making a simple meal

In successfully completing this module

....

has demonstrated that he/she

1. can make a realistic meal choice with support, e.g.:

2. can put together a shopping list for the meal, e.g.:

3. can take part in a shopping expedition and recognise some of the ingredients for the meal on the shelves, e.g.:

4. can find some of the appropriate equipment from the kitchen after discussion, e.g.:

5. can set a place setting at the table for their meal; comment:

6. can use appropriately some of the key words: (please tick)
   dinner ☐   list ☐   shopping ☐   place setting ☐

Figure 7.5 Certificate of Achievement showing teaching stages for Module 4

Breakfast foods (module 6)

This module will enable pupils to develop the concept of the value of a healthy breakfast. Pupils will be given the opportunity to prepare a simple breakfast, look at different breakfast cereals and develop skills to look for healthy options. Pupils will make a survey of what people like for breakfast and make a chart to illustrate this. Pupils will have the opportunity to make a hot drink and to use the toaster. Pupils will develop safety skills for use in the kitchen.

The teaching stages are listed on the Certificate of Achievement for this module (see Figure 7.6).

Food Technology
Certificate of Achievement

Module Number 6
Breakfast foods

In successfully completing this module

....

has demonstrated that he/she

1. can take part in a survey to discover what people eat for breakfast

2. can recognise 'breakfast' foods, e.g.:

3. can do a taste test on various cereals and say which they like, e.g.:

4. am developing skills for 'healthy' breakfast recognition

5. can make toast: comment;

6. can make a hot drink: comment;

7. can recognise some key words: (please tick)

    cereal ☐   toast ☐   drink ☐   sugar ☐

8. can collect the appropriate equipment

Figure 7.6 Certificate of Achievement showing teaching stages for Module 6

Stage 1: I can take part in a survey to discover what people eat for breakfast

The concept is: healthy breakfast foods. The aim is that pupils begin to understand the concept of a healthy breakfast. There are cross-curricular links to Mathematics and English – Speaking and Listening.

☞ **Activity**
Do a breakfast food survey of pupils and adults in the class, i.e. find out what people eat for breakfast and record results on a simple graph chart. Discuss the types and popularity of the various breakfast foods on the chart.

Words used: hot/cold, cereal, fresh, low sugar, fibre, bread, like/dislike, choose, names of breakfast foods.
Resources: clip board, paper and pen for survey; large sheet of paper and pens to record results of survey.

Stages 4, 5 and 6: I can make toast and a hot drink, and am developing skills for 'healthy' breakfast recognition

The concept is: healthy breakfast foods. The aim is that pupils practise simple preparation skills, and begin to look for and recognise 'healthy' options.

☞ **Activity**
Organise a session to make a hot drink and fresh orange juice, also toast using a toaster. Using pictures from magazines and real packets, look at a range of breakfast cereals and choose those with low sugar. (Some can be tasted and discussed.)

Words used: juice, toaster, fibre, low energy, like/dislike, low fat spread.
Resources: pictures of relevant breakfast foods for magazines, a range of cereals to taste, toaster, juice, bread.

Food groups: vitamins (module 8)

This module will enable pupils to name fruit and vegetables, to group both fruit and vegetables and to match them. It will also introduce the concept of 'vitamins'. It will enable pupils to develop skills of making an informed choice on healthy eating type foods. Pupils will make posters of fruits and vegetables, and make various recipes from fruit and vegetables. Pupils will develop the skills necessary for the preparation of fruit and vegetables ready for eating.

The teaching stages are shown in the Certificate of Achievement for this module (see Figure 7.7).

Stage 3: I can say what vitamins fruit and vegetables give us (vitamin C)

The concept is: names and groups of vegetables containing vitamin C. The aim is to teach pupils about health-giving vitamin C. There are cross-curricular links with English – Speaking and Listening.

☞ **Activity**
Using pictures from magazines or pupils' own drawings, make a poster of fruits and vegetables which are high in vitamin C. Discuss why vitamin C is important for the body.

Food Technology
Certificate of Achievement

Module Number 8
Food Groups (Vitamins)

In successfully completing this module

....

has demonstrated that he/she

1. can recognise and name some fruits, e.g.:

2. can recognise and name some vegetables, e.g.:

3. can say what vitamins fruit and vegetables give us (vitamin C)

4. can make up fruit and vegetable dishes with appropriate support, e.g.:

5. can match fruits to fruits and vegetables to vegetables and also group them generically, e.g.:

6. has developed key preparation skills:
   washing ☐   peeling   ☐ chopping ☐   cutting   ☐

7. can use appropriate key vocabulary
   fruit names ☐   vegetable names ☐   vitamin ☐

Figure 7.7 Certificate of Achievement showing teaching stages for Module 8

☞ **Activity**
Make a fresh fruit salad using fruits which are high in vitamin C, emphasising that there is more vitamin C in fresh, uncooked fruit and vegetables.

Words used: vitamin C, food group, fresh, healthy, fight infections, names of fruits high in vitamin C (e.g. blackcurrants, citrus fruits), juice.

Resources: magazines containing pictures of fruit and vegetables; large sheet of paper and glue; fruit, bowl, chopping board, knife and spoons.

Healthy eating (module 10)

To develop skills to recognise 'healthy' food, concentrating particularly on low fat food. Pupils will sort foods into red and green categories, using real objects and photographs. They will have opportunities to make healthy snacks, and visit the tuck shop to choose healthy alternatives. Pupils will build up knowledge to help them develop informed choices for healthy food. Pupils will look for the 'healthy eating' symbol on packaging and they will produce a list of healthy snack choices.

The teaching stages are shown on the Certificate of Achievement for this module (see Figure 7.8).

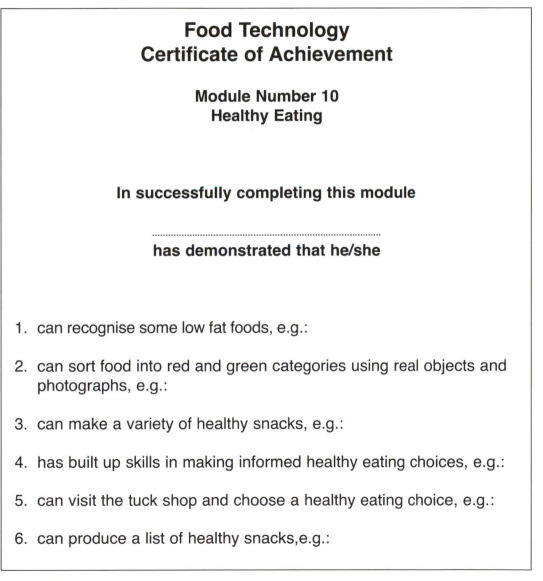

Food Technology
Certificate of Achievement

Module Number 10
Healthy Eating

In successfully completing this module

....

has demonstrated that he/she

1. can recognise some low fat foods, e.g.:

2. can sort food into red and green categories using real objects and photographs, e.g.:

3. can make a variety of healthy snacks, e.g.:

4. has built up skills in making informed healthy eating choices, e.g.:

5. can visit the tuck shop and choose a healthy eating choice, e.g.:

6. can produce a list of healthy snacks,e.g.:

Figure 7.8 Certificate of Achievement showing teaching stages for Module 10

Stages 1 and 4: I can recognise some low fat foods, and choose a healthy eating choice

The concept is: low fat foods. The aim is to develop an understanding of foods which are good (and which are not so good) for us.

☞ **Activity**
To recognise some low fat foods, pupils visit the school tuck shop and choose a healthy eating choice for their break.

☞ **Activity**
Healthy snacks: have a 'brainstorming' session. Pupils call out their ideas, which the teacher writes on a large sheet of paper. Pupils then choose one of these ideas for a snack to make.

Words used: healthy, low fat, sugar/salt, sandwich, food names such as popcorn and fruit.

Resources: school tuck shop or local shops, toaster, cooker, cooking utensils, healthy choices snacks such as popcorn, toast, vegetable 'sticks' etc.

Notes on an *Attitudes to Food* workshop

At Piper Hill, when developing our curriculum, we examined and explored our attitudes though a staff workshop (Figure 7.9). This brought out many issues for discussion as follows.

How as a school do we abuse food?

These points need consideration:

- reward/removal of reward
- using snacks as a calming activity
- treats
- waste – unused leftovers/at lunchtime
- lack of choice/choice
- punishments/denial
- fried food portrayed as smiling faces
- expectation of a biscuit at break time
- overeating, e.g. after food tech lesson then straight to dinner
- dirty handling
- greed/parties
- too much/too little

Food and health

Here are some points to remember:

- a balanced diet is essential in childhood to meet physical needs
- eating patterns/attitudes towards food are established in childhood
- disease processes may commence in childhood

- diets of British children tend to be high in fat and sugar and low in calcium, iron and fibre
- research has recognised clearer links between dietary factors and the risk of various illnesses and disease.

Coronary heart disease is the major cause of death in England. The mortality rates for both men and women in Manchester are higher than the rates for England and Wales (82/100,000 compared to 45/100,000 Mancunian Community Health NHS Trust, 1997). The underlying process which leads to the narrowing of arteries begins in childhood. Lifestyles and behaviours which can increase the risk of heart disease are learned and begin early in life.

Obesity is a problem among both adults and children in the UK. It is a result of high calorie intake (eating too much). Obesity is a health risk: there is increased risk of stroke, heart disease, high blood pressure and diabetes. An overweight adolescent tends to become an obese adult and many normal weight children will become overweight by middle age. How many overweight children are there in our school?

Dental caries – tooth decay

Manchester has the highest incidence of tooth decay in England and Wales (67 per cent of South Manchester under fives and 75 per cent of North Manchester under fives have decayed, missing or filled teeth; North West Dental Public Health Resource Centre, 1997). The most important fact in determining the rate of dental decay is the number of times that sugars enter the mouth. Sugars should be consumed as part of a meal rather than in between meals. Snacks and drinks should be free of sugar and the frequent consumption of acidic drinks should be avoided.

The situation at Piper Hill High School

- There are children with weight problems.
- Dental problems are frequent amongst Manchester children and dental care may be difficult for our children.
- Snacks between meals are the problem – snacks can't be treated as a one off.
- Parents may be struggling at home to maintain a sensible diet and say no to snacks.
- We must be consistent and provide continuity for the child, especially as often the pupils are more cooperative in school and it is easier for us.
- Many children are difficult about food at home: tantrums, stealing etc.
- We need to be clear in our message about healthy eating.

Don't despair! Food should still be fun if the subject is presented in a positive way at school, i.e. food technology lessons, helping to make healthy choices, tuck shop, lunch, celebrations, birthdays, religious festivals, tasting, sharing.

We achieved the Gold Healthy School Award which is ours for three years. We have set a standard and need to maintain it.

'Attitudes to Food'

Exploring Our Attitudes and Defining Important Issues about Food and our Pupils

A Workshop Plan
Healthy Eating Messages

Brainstorm – all messages	5 mins

Eat less fat, give me five, eat more fibre, eat less sugar etc. How many of us know the messages, but do we do it?

Our feelings around food	7 mins

Divide into small groups

Write down our feelings around food, i.e. comfort, reward, happiness, celebration, treats etc.

Report back – write up new messages from each group.

Processing feedback – need to eat for health, energy etc. Lots of reasons – emotional satisfaction, eating = control, rewards.   7 mins

At school we need to look at this.

How as a school do we use/ abuse food?	

In department groups fill in a sheet on this   7 mins

Take feedback – write up all comments in two columns
(use/abuse food)   10 mins

What are the important points for health?	5 mins

Links with Coronary Heart Disease – this begins in childhood, obesity

Manchester (especially Wythenshawe) has the worst record of bad teeth in children. Sugary snacks between meals are a cause of caries. We have Gold Healthy School Award for three years and need to set a standard

Good practice in Manchester schools	5 mins

Examples of practical work in other schools as documented for the Healthy School Award

Figure 7.9 Piper Hill's workshop for staff led by the PSE coordinator and the school nurse

Good practice in Manchester schools

- **Breakfast Clubs**, some combined with exercise, aim to improve attendance, health, good habits and behaviour. Quite a few primary and some secondaries now have them.
- **Tuck Shops** have become fruit only shops in a couple of schools and many others are aiming for healthier snacks. Some schools ban sweets and crisps.
- **Health Weeks** are popular in the secondary sector.
- **Gardening** One inner city secondary school has an allotment, where pupils garden with students from the university. Some primary schools grow produce for example, the Super Carrot Project at one primary school, and an Orchard and Herb garden at another.

Where it is a success, schools consult and make changes with the whole school. They consult and work with city catering, staff, parents and pupils to make changes. One local secondary school provides healthy alternatives in the canteen as well as having a breakfast club which is combined with exercise.

In the new phase of the Healthy School Award, which has just been launched, more schools are looking at healthy eating and issues around food.

Chapter 8

Personal Hygiene

It is essential that all pupils know why personal hygiene is important and that they are able to keep themselves clean, tidy and fit. They need to understand that personal cleanliness helps to reduce risks of disease, and should be encouraged to take pride in looking after themselves.

For those pupils totally dependent on adult care it is important to include personal hygiene and cleanliness in their daily routine. For some pupils it is appropriate to encourage a degree of cooperation in this activity, but for others it will be a passive activity that nevertheless is an essential part of their curriculum.

In the area of Personal Hygiene, close links between home and school are necessary. They can be built up by means of:

- certificates (see Figures 8.3, 8.4, 8.6 and 8.7)
- the Annual Review
- home/school diaries (if these are used by the school)
- letters to inform and engage parents in activities (see Figure 8.5)
- meetings with parents and carers (such as coffee mornings), which can be arranged for a variety of purposes, such as encouraging independence, gaining awards in schools such as those offered by ASDAN.

The contents of the Personal Hygiene curriculum at Piper Hill is shown in Figure 8.1. Pupils work on Personal Hygiene every day as part of their ongoing individual targets, and teachers pick out appropriate tasks for each pupil from the lists given in this chapter under the headings Personal care, Showering and Dental care (see Figure 8.2). Note that the ASDAN Award – choosing a daily routine – is done only in Key Stage 4, and Careers and Personal Care only in the FE Department.

Certificates

Certificates serve several functions. They make a useful check-list for the teacher, but they also serve as an encouragement for the pupils to take charge of their own learning. When a certificate, or part of the certificate, is completed it can act as a record of learning in the pupil's own Record of Achievement (an individual pupil record at Piper Hill, based on the national Record of Achievement). Certificates also serve as a home–school link. Learning is more effective if home and school can

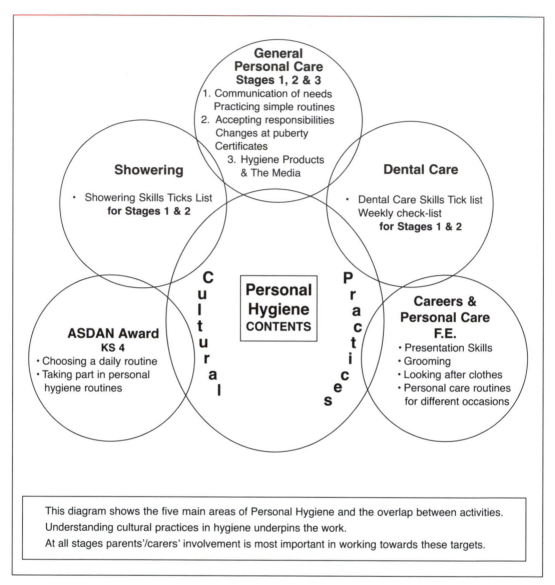

Figure 8.1 Personal Hygiene curriculum at Piper Hill

work together on personal hygiene tasks. These hygiene tasks are often discussed at a pupil's Annual Review (a requirement by law for pupils with a Statement of Special Needs where a meeting is held annually between school and the parent/carer). Here the certificate could be used as part of the pupil's contribution to the review and as a planner for identifying targets for the pupil's learning the following year.

TERMLY PLANNING SHEET				
Term Autumn	**Year** 1996	**Curriculum Area** PSE	**Class** S1	**N.C. Year** 7

SOURCE: Piper Hill PSE Curriculum   A Personal Hygiene B Body Parts

AIMS: **Personal Hygiene:**   • to be able to keep ourselves clean, tidy and fit
• to reduce risks of disease
• to take pride in looking after ourselves

         Body Parts   • to be aware of changes and to cope with them
• to name and understand body parts

SPECIFIC TEACHING POINTS/OBJECTIVES.

A • The importance of privacy – changing and washing.
   • Teeth cleaning – how to clean properly; when and why important – to carry out at home. Report back next day if teeth were cleaned.
   • Foods good/bad for teeth. Posters, collections, displays.
   • Select appropriate hygiene items, e.g. I am going to wash my hair; what do I need? Wash hair: can you do it by yourself? When do we wash, use deodorants? Have own toilet bag.

B • Differences between girl, boy, teenager, man, woman, mum, dad, grandma.

     Vocabulary: breast, nipple, penis, vagina etc.
     Privacy during lessons

ACTIVITIES/RESOURCES USED.

A • Make a group collage of hygiene products – recognise names – sight reading.
   • Visit from dental nurses – pictures, models, brushes, floss, mouthwash, disclosure tablets.
   • Shopping trip to buy floss, tablets, toothbrushes, cleansers, shampoo – buy a toilet bag for each pupil.
   • Hygiene bag – feel/chosen item – what is it? What do I do with it?
   • TV adverts – can you guess what it is for? Do you use it at home? e.g. shampoo, soap, Persil, deodorant, body foam.

B • On the Agenda (Scott et al., 1994) ideas: look at line drawings of children at different stages – what age is this person? What can she do?
   • Circle game: Touch your head, toes, cheeks, nipples – breast – 'no that's private'. Importance of privacy at school and at home.

CROSS-CURRICULAR LINKS:

   PE
   Science
   English – Speaking and Listening

Figure 8.2 Termly planning for personal hygiene

Personal care (module 1)

Stage 1: Communication and practice

At this stage, pupils should understand the need and be able to practice simple routines such as washing hands, cleaning teeth, using a handkerchief;
- ☐ I can make myself-clean and tidy.
- ☐ I can make myself-look smart.
- ☐ I can use the toilet without any help.
- ☐ I can wash my hands and dry them.
- ☐ I can brush and comb my hair, looking in the mirror.
- ☐ I clean my teeth after meals without any help and I remember it myself.
- ☐ I know when and how to wipe my nose.
- ☐ I can dress and undress myself.
- ☐ I can keep myself-clean and tidy.
- ☐ I can begin to understand that some diseases are infectious and that transmission may be reduced by the use of simple, safe routines.
- ☐ I know I can catch certain illnesses from others, e.g. chicken pox, a cold.
- ☐ I know that if I have an infectious illness I should keep away from others until I am better.
- ☐ I know that if I am very ill, I must stay at home and rest until I feel better
- ☐ I know what I must do if I feel ill, e.g. sleep, take medicine.

Pupils with Profound and Multiple Learning Disabilities

At Stage 1, pupils with PMLD should be able to communicate when feeling ill by crying, facial and body gestures, vocalising the need for toileting, accepting hands being washed, and so on:
(Toileting)
- ☐ I accept being taken to the bathroom and cooperate when my pads are changed.
- ☐ I cooperate when taken to the toilet and will sometimes use it appropriately.
- ☐ I can stay clean and dry for a day if taken regularly to the toilet by an adult.
- ☐ I can stay clean and dry for long periods.

(Hand washing/bathing/showering/teeth brushing).
- ☐ I accept having my hands and face washed and dried.
- ☐ I cooperate when I'm given a bath or shower.
- ☐ I accept having my teeth cleaned if it is done gently.
- ☐ I cooperate when having my hair combed and brushed.
- ☐ I allow my nose to be wiped when it is necessary.
- ☐ I allow my limbs to be moved (i.e. I don't resist) when being dressed.
- ☐ I help a little when I'm dressed by holding out my arms and legs.

At Piper Hill, we have used the shadow puppet workshops run by Elizabeth Gamlin (Gamlin, 1994) to further awareness at this stage, in particular *Outside/Inside*, which is designed to develop awareness of germs and viruses and how they get into the body (including HIV). The workshops are tailored to meet pupils' level of knowledge and skills, and do it very successfully.

Stage 2: Accepting responsibilities

At Stage 2, pupils should understand the needs and, where allowed to, accept responsibility for personal cleanliness:

☐ I wash my hands before meals and after using the toilet.
☐ I comb my hair.
☐ I can wash and dry my hair.
☐ I can scrub my nails and know why they need cutting.
☐ I brush my teeth.
☐ I wash and dry my face.

Pupils with Profound and Multiple Learning Disabilities

☐ I accept being helped to be clean and tidy.
☐ I cooperate with being helped to look smart.
☐ I enjoy the feeling of being clean and comfortable.
☐ I like looking in the mirror when my hair has been washed and dried.

Changes at puberty

In addition at this stage, pupils should know and understand how changes at puberty affect the body in relation to hygiene:

☐ I know I need to bath or shower more regularly to keep my body clean and healthy.
☐ I know I need to use a deodorant daily to make me smell fresh and clean.
☐ I know how to cleanse my skin on my face.
☐ (Girls) I understand about my periods and know how to change my pad.

Certificate in Personal Hygiene

Pupils will be encouraged to demonstrate that they can achieve as many stages as possible in the Certificate in Personal Hygiene (see Figures 8.3 and 8.4). To achieve this parents and carers help their child to work through several tasks at home, e.g. 'can help with household tasks at home' (Figure 8.5).

Stage 2: I understand why hand washing is important

The concept is: infections can be spread by our hands. The aim is that pupils understand that hand washing stops us getting ill. There are cross-curricular links to English, Speaking and Listening, and to Art.

☞ **Activity**
   Present a drama about hand washing, to show that dirty hands can make you ill. The teacher plays the part of mum, who prepares tea with dirty hands (use eyebrow pencil to depict dirt/germs). Two children eat their tea and later that night are very sick. Repeat the drama: this time mum washes her hands and the children stay well. Let the pupils play the scene again, taking different roles. Discuss what happens.

☞ **Activity**
   Poster-making competition: the pupils draw or write something that they have learnt about the importance of hand washing on a large sheet of paper. The school nurse chooses the best entry from each year group and these are laminated and displayed in strategic places, such as the toilets, to remind pupils to wash their hands.

A Certificate in Personal Hygiene (Girls)

Name:..   Date:............................

• I blow my nose and dispose of the tissue
• I brush and comb my hair
• I can tie my hair back and keep it tidy
• I know when to wash my hands – e.g., before dinner, after using the toilet
• I flush the toilet and leave it tidy
• I scrub my nails and know when they need cutting
• I know the importance of keeping my body clean, using deodorants when necessary
• I wash my hair using the correct temperature of water
• I clean the bath and shower afterwards
• I know how to use facial cleansers to help to prevent spots
• I cope discretely with my period
• I understand the importance of keeping my teeth clean
• I brush my teeth at home
• I can select appropriate items for looking after myself, e.g. toothbrush, shampoo, sanitary towel, soaps, cleansers, moisturisers, sun-cream, toe-nail clippers, nail brush, dental floss, toilet paper, 'bug-buster' comb
• I clean my glasses and look after them sensibly
• I know how to 'bug-bust' (check for headlice)
• I know when my clothes need changing
• I can dress sensibly for appropriate occasions, e.g. hot, cold, evening, sport, working etc.
• I can clean up after myself, e.g. wash up dirty cups, wipe down table, clean shoes
• I can help with household tasks at home

Figure 8.3 A certificate is a record of learning

A Certificate in Personal Hygiene (Boys)
Name:... Date:.................................
• I blow my nose and dispose of the tissue
• I brush and comb my hair
• I know when to wash my hands – e.g. before dinner, after using the toilet
• I flush the toilet and leave it tidy
• I scrub my nails and know when they need cutting
• I know the importance of keeping my body clean, using deodorants when necessary
• I wash my hair using the correct temperature of water
• I clean the bath and shower afterwards
• I know how to use facial cleansers to help to prevent spots
• I understand the importance of keeping my teeth clean
• I brush my teeth at home
• I can select appropriate items for looking after myself, e.g. toothbrush, shampoo, shaving cream, soaps, cleansers, moisturisers, sun-cream, toe-nail clippers, nail brush, dental floss, toilet paper, 'bug-buster' comb
• I clean my glasses and look after them sensibly
• I know how to 'bug-bust' (check for headlice)
• I know when my clothes need changing
• I can dress sensibly for appropriate occasions, e.g. hot, cold, evening, sport, working etc.
• I can clean up after myself, e.g. wash up dirty cups, wipe down table, clean shoes
• I can help with household tasks at home

Figure 8.4 A certificate is also a checklist

Manchester City Council Education Department

PIPER HILL HIGH SCHOOL

200, Yew Tree Lane   Headteacher:
Northenden   Jenny Andrews
Manchester M23 0FF

Tel: 0161 998 4068
Fax: 0161 945 6625

Dear Parents and Carers,

This half term .... has been working on a Health Certificate on Personal Hygiene.
We would be really glad of your help in completing some of the tasks at home.
If possible over the next two weeks, could ....

        1.

        2.

        3.

We have left a blank on the certificate for you to initial and sign when the tasks are completed and then could you send the certificate back to school for a presentation.

Thank you for your help.

Yours sincerely,

Linda Otten

Figure 8.5 Engaging parents/carers in activities is essential

Words used: washing, hands, clean/dirty, infection, germs, ill, sickness, after (using the toilet), before (eating).

Resources: props for drama (table, pans and plates); food, eyebrow pencil or dark eye shadow; paints, felt tip pens and large sheets of paper for poster making.

Stage 3: Hygiene products and the media

The concept is: how hygiene products are portrayed in TV advertisements. The aim is for pupils to recognise different types of hygiene products and their uses. There are cross-curricular links to ASDAN-Science Positive Self-Image Activity KS4 (see Figure 11.3, Chapter 11).

☞ **Activity**
The teacher collects several adverts for hygiene products on a video tape (the pupils could help to make the video by identifying hygiene product adverts and recording them). Pupils watch the video and talk about the adverts. They say which products they like, and why. The pupils could also compare the prices of these products.

☞ **Activity**
Look at a general video of current adverts. Discuss why we have adverts. Pupils then try to make up an advert for a hygiene product that they think would help sell it.

Words used: advert, hygiene, deodorant, perfume, aftershave, soap.

Resources: a video of hygiene adverts, a video of general current adverts.

Showering (module 2)

All stages are shown on the showering skills chart (Figure 8.6). This is because some pupils at 11 years will complete the sheet whilst others will only work at parts of it and will continue this work throughout their whole school career. The idea is that pupils take it home and fill it in with their parent/carer. Thus it serves a similar function to the certificates.

Dental care (module 3)

It is recommended that schools work with the Dental Health Team from their local area, who will visit the school and run sessions with the pupils to improve their knowledge and understanding of teeth care. They will also identify specific students who may need individual programmes of teeth brushing; but for all it is ongoing work.

The dental care skills chart (Figure 8.7) provides a check-list of skills, and serves a similar function to the certificates. The idea is that the pupils take the skills chart and the toothbrushing chart (Figure 8.8) home to fill in with the parent/carer.

Stage 1: I understand how to keep my teeth and mouth clean

The concept is: a clean and healthy mouth. The aim is for pupils to learn to brush correctly and take responsibility for oral hygiene.

Showering Skills							
Name:....................................							
Date							
1. I have brought the right things for a shower: towel, deodorant, soap/shower gel, hair brush/comb							
2. I can undress myself completely after PE							
3. I know how to get undressed in private							
4. I can turn on the shower							
5. I can restart the shower when the water stops							
6. I can use soap/shower gel to wash under my arms							
7. I can use soap/shower gel to wash between my legs							
8. I know when to stop showering							
9. I can keep my clothes and towel dry whilst showering							
10. I can dry myself – under my arms							
11. I can dry myself – between my legs							
12. I can dry myself – between my toes							
13. I can put deodorant under my arms							
14. I can put on my underwear first							
15. I can finish dressing myself – apart from my shoes							
16. I can fasten my shoes							
17. I can collect up together my towel, deodorant, soap/shower gel and hairbrush							
18. I can collect up together my PE kit							
19. I can leave the shower/changing room clean and tidy							
✓ ✓ = achieve unaided ✓ = achieve with support							

Figure 8.6 The showering skills chart is a form of certificate

Dental Care Skills								
Name:.......................................								
Date								
1. I hold my toothbrush								
2. I unscrew the toothpaste lid								
3. I put a small blob of toothpaste on my brush								
4. I brush my front teeth								
5. I brush my back teeth								
6. I brush my top teeth								
7. I brush my bottom teeth								
8. I brush my lower left teeth								
9. I brush my lower right teeth								
10. I brush my upper left teeth								
11. I brush my upper right teeth								
12. I rinse my mouth								
13. I rinse my brush								
14. I turn the cold tap on/off								
15. I brush my teeth with help								
16. I brush my teeth on my own								
17. I remember to brush my teeth myself								
18. I know why I brush my teeth								
✓ ✓ = achieve unaided ✓ = achieve with support								

Figure 8.7 The check-list of skills also registers achievement

Toothbrushing Chart

Please tick ✓ when you have brushed your teeth

	Morning	Night
Monday		
Tuesday		
Wednesday		
Thursday		
Friday		
Saturday		
Sunday		

This is a correct record of ....'s
toothbrushing this week   (child's name)

Signed ....
(Parent/Carer)

Figure 8.8 The chart is taken home and completed with the parent/carer

☞ **Activity**
Start a discussion on teeth, what they are used for; first and second teeth. Teach some practical teeth cleaning – each pupil to have a go. Individual programmes may have to be considered and amended. Emphasise the importance of the use of own brush.

☞ **Activity**
Start a discussion on why we should clean our teeth. Practise teeth cleaning and the use of a mouthwash.

Words used: toothbrush, toothpaste, tap, water, sink, glass, mouthwash.
Resources: toothbrushes, toothpaste, mouthwash, toothbrushing charts.

Careers and personal care (module 5)

This is a six-week module followed by pupils in the FE Department at Piper Hilland is not within the scope of this book, although the following outline may be of interest:

- Personal hygiene and presentation skills
- Preparation for an interview
- A visit to a local college beauty therapy department
- The importance of hygiene and good grooming
- Looking after clothes, including washing
- Hygiene routines for different events, such as sport or a special occasion
- Facials, a manicure, use of the foot spa and massage oils.

Cultural practices in personal hygiene (Muslim)

As stated earlier (Figure 8.1), cultural practices in hygiene underpin our work at Piper Hill. We have a number of Muslim pupils at school whose faith places great importance on hygiene. We wanted to ensure that we were addressing their needs, in the same way that we would endeavour to meet the cultural needs of other pupils. We have a teacher who works on liaison between school and home of ethnic minority students.

It is our current practice at Piper Hill to work closely with all parents/carers on issues which are part of their faith and lives. Opportunities for consultation take place formally at medicals and annual reviews, and then through informal contacts with the school nurse and teachers. As far as possible we try to meet conditions for Muslim cleanliness and in some cases, as a result of parental consultation, pupils take part in a specific hygiene programme, e.g. training in washing or using wet wipes after using the toilet.

Prayer

Many Muslims pray five times a day (dawn – *Fajr*, at midday – *Zuhr*, late afternoon – *Asr*, after sunset – *Maghrib*, and late evening before going to bed – *Ishà*). Before prayer all Muslims must wash. This is a ritual washing, an act of purification – ablution (*wudhû*).

Ablution includes washing the hands, gargling, rinsing the mouth and nostrils, washing the face, the arms, passing wet hands over the hair and, lastly, washing the feet. A normal wash-basin will do. Muslims prefer to wash in running water, that is, they would prefer a shower to a bath. A bowl or bucket and jug, wet wipes or a bidet would also be suitable. Menstruating women do not enter the mosque.

Toilet/washing facilities

Many Muslims regard the use of toilet paper as insufficient in terms of hygiene and wash with water after using the toilet. A cleansing vessel is used for this purpose. This is a simple vessel which has a long spout. A plastic jug or wet wipes may also be used and are available for use in school. As a rule Muslims use their left hand for toileting and their right hand for eating, but it is now acceptable for left-handed people to eat with their left hand (of course hand washing is still important).

Changing facilities

Muslims require separate changing areas for PE and also showering facilities. This includes individual cubicles. It is common for males to cover their bodies from navel to knees and females from head to foot, leaving only face and hands uncovered. It is embarrassing to undress in front of others and to shower alongside someone else: this is forbidden by Islam. For communal showers Muslim boys and girls might wear appropriate clothing to cover their private parts.

Pupils' study unit

☐ I know and understand that Muslims wash before praying.
☐ I know that ablution (*wudhû*) is a ritual act of washing/purification before prayer.
☐ I know that ablution involves washing different parts of the body: washing the hands, gargling, rinsing the mouth and nostrils, washing the face, washing the arms, passing wet hands over the hair, washing the feet.
☐ I know that Muslims prefer to wash in running water, e.g. would prefer a shower to a bath.
☐ I know and understand that cleanliness is an important part of the Faith.

☞ **Activity**
A visit to a Mosque would help illustrate some of the above, e.g. pupils would see low wash-basins specially designed for washing feet.

☐ I know and understand that Muslims wash with water after using the toilet.
☐ I understand that many Muslims would regard the use of toilet paper insufficient in terms of hygiene, therefore wash with water or use a wet wipe.
☐ I know that other Asian cultures and Western European cultures also wash with water after using the toilet (e.g. using a bidet).

☐ I know that a simple vessel with a long spout is traditionally used for washing.

☐ I know that Muslims use their left hand for toileting (right hand can hold toileting jug).

☐ I know and understand that Muslim men must cover their bodies from navel to knee.

☐ I know and understand that Muslim women must dress modestly.

☐ I know that Muslim males and females require separate changing facilities, showers and PE/swimming lessons; they also prefer single-sex education at secondary age.

Chapter 9

Environmental Aspects of Health Education

The general aim of this topic is to develop in pupils an understanding of the influences on our environment, and of how the way we live can affect our health. The chapter gives an outline of suggested activities at Key Stages 3 and 4. However, this is an area of the Personal and Social Education curriculum which is addressed mainly through the following curriculum links at Piper Hill:

- the PE curriculum, and the experience and knowledge that exercise is good for health;
- the Food Technology curriculum and the links with healthy eating (see Chapter 7, modules 2 and 10);
- the Personal Hygiene curriculum (module 1);
- the FE curriculum (outlined at Figure 1.3, pp8–9) on Citizenship and gaining insights into the lifestyles of others;
- the RE curriculum, which includes sections on the Natural World – Responsibility and Choices, and Understanding other Faiths and Cultures.

A balanced healthy lifestyle (module 1)

Work relating to this module may be undertaken via PE, Food Technology (Chapter 7, modules 2 and 10), and health education. Pupils will:

- develop a knowledge of the importance of exercise for good health;
- develop a knowledge of healthy eating patterns through Food Technology topics;
- develop a knowledge of, and an interest in, various forms of exercise through school activities, e.g. gym club; swimming; team games; routines in PE, walking out of doors;
- develop an interest in and a liking for a healthy balanced diet through cookery and mini-enterprise sessions (introducing new dishes in an attractive way) and through eating out (broadening pupils' knowledge of fast food available by visiting a variety of establishments, and trying dishes that are compatible with a balanced healthy diet).

Activities should aim to develop an eating lifestyle that doesn't exclude anything, and therefore can continue long term. Much discussion will take place on the idea of what is a 'balanced' diet. Pupils' ideas of balance will vary. Within the study of a 'balanced' diet, introduce variety, e.g. foods from a wide variety of countries and cultures; foods that have a religious significance; vegetarian foods.

The spread of diseases (module 2)

The main objective is that pupils learn to distinguish between infectious and non-infectious diseases, know how they are spread and assist in their prevention. The programme begins by looking at what a germ is, how germs spread, and how they make us ill (see Chapter 8, module 1). Another way of introducing the topic and beginning discussion is to use the *Outside/Inside* puppet workshop (Gamlin, 1994).

In all schools there are some common and easily spread infections such as colds and 'flu, cold sores, head lice, verrucae: pupils learn first about how these are spread. Methods of controlling spread, such as using a handkerchief, need to be taught at an early stage.

Routines for dealing with cuts and grazes may be demonstrated on yourself and the importance of not touching anyone else's blood, to prevent the spread of infection, must be stressed.

Illnesses such as measles, chicken pox, mumps etc. should be discussed and pupils will learn that these illnesses are infectious. But they must also understand that some people will become ill and even die from conditions that are not infectious.

For the teaching plan, refer to module 1 of Chapter 8; Personal Hygiene.

The influence of the media (module 3)

The aims of this module are that pupils understand the impact of the media and advertising on attitudes towards health and that they are aware of the areas that may be strongly influenced by their presentation in the media (see Chapter 8, module 1, stage 3). The main areas are:

- diet, where huge sums are spent promoting low fat 'healthy' foods and crash diets marketed as 'miracle cures';
- smoking, as presented on TV programmes and advertised on bill boards;
- exercise, in particular the way in which trainers and sports wear are advertised as an aid to increased athleticism.

Stage 1: The impact of the media and advertising on attitudes towards health

The concepts are: diet, low fat, calories, advert, body sizes and weight. The aim is to understand how advertisements for different diets affect the pupils' attitudes to health. There are cross-curricular links to PSE Food and Nutrition.

☞ **Activity**
Collect different diet and low fat products, and those marketed as 'miracle cures', to compare and discuss. Talk about the necessity, cost and nutritional value of these products.

☞ **Activity**
Collect advertisements for low fat, diet type products. Study the people in adverts – are they men or women? What are they doing? What do they look like? Discuss whether one product could make you look like this. Talk about which foods the pupils choose to buy.

Words used: diet, low fat, calorie, calorie controlled, slim, energy, fit, healthy, flavour, cost.
Resources: collection of low fat, diet type products; advertisements from magazines and TV on this theme.

Stage 2: The impact of the media and advertising on attitudes towards health

The concepts are: advertising, exercise, sportswear, different sports activities, health and fitness. The aim is to understand how trainers and sportswear are advertised as an aid to increased athleticism. There are cross-curricular links with PE and English.

☞ **Activity**
Collect magazine advertisements for sportswear. In the group, discuss who the people in the adverts are and what they are wearing. What do the people look like? Ask the pupils if they would like to look like this.

☞ **Activity**
Look at magazine advertisements again or TV video clips of sports gear advertisements. Which sportswear items do the pupils like? Why? What would they choose to buy, and what activities would they do whilst wearing the chosen item?

Words used: trainers, shorts, shirts, advert, exercise, strong, fast, muscle, speed, fit, healthy, running, jumping, grip, power.
Resources: advertisements for sportswear from magazines; video of TV adverts for sportswear.

Taking responsibility (module 4)

In Key Stage 4, the aim is to enable pupils to take responsibility for their health and lifestyle, and to be aware that people's attitudes and lifestyles differ. Pupils look at food distribution and the effect of famine and over-consumption on health. Pupils work together towards developing a commitment to their own health care, and to that of other people. The statements addressed in Key Stage 4 are that pupils should:

- accept responsibility for and be able to justify personal choices and decisions about health;
- show some insight into other people's lifestyles, values, attitudes and decisions;
- be aware of how food shortages and surpluses occur, and the health effects of malnutrition and over-consumption;
- develop commitment to the care and improvement of their own and other people's health, community and environment.

A useful source book for activities on these themes is Burns and Lamont (1995), in particular The Coffee Quiz , where pupils are encouraged to think about where food comes from; Newcomers, which explores how we treat one another; and The Hoop, an activity which helps pupils appreciate the world around them.

Accepting responsibility

Having followed programmes relating to KS3 on developing a healthy lifestyle, pupils will be able to take on some responsibility for their own health; to make informed choices about what they eat; what exercise they take; whether or not they drink alcohol.

Developing insight into other people's lifestyles

Through Careers and Citizenship programmes contained in the FE curriculum (outlined in Figure 1.3), students will look at natural disasters such as famine, and will learn about how the health of the population is affected.

Food shortages and surpluses

Pupils will learn about the distribution of wealth throughout the world, and how the health of the population is affected by excess as well as famine.

Care of health, community and environment

Pupils develop a commitment to the care of the school and home environment by not becoming involved in acts of vandalism, and by taking an active part in the care of their school, e.g. by picking up litter, keeping rooms tidy, being aware of room temperature and opening windows where necessary.

Through involvement in the RE curriculum they develop an awareness of need in the world, e.g. Christian Aid Week, Red Nose Day, delivering Harvest time parcels to elderly people in the locality; and they organise special projects to help with a particular problem, e.g. collecting socks for homeless people.

Chapter 10

Advocacy

Developing self-esteem

All schools should be working towards developing pupils' self-esteem, because this is the foundation of good self-advocacy. Pupils who can build up a positive self-image, with an awareness of their skills and worth, and who learn to cope with negative experiences, are far better able to be assertive about their needs and choices.

Self-esteem is fostered by helping pupils to:

- recognise and develop individual strengths
- accept failures and mistakes
- improve in areas where they are weak
- feel comfortable with themselves
- develop positive relationships
- take part in activities they enjoy
- create some successes.

Self-advocacy skills

It is important to identify the self-advocacy skills which the school aims to encourage. These will include the pupils' being able to:

- say 'YES' and 'NO'
- communicate feelings
- be assertive
- understand their human rights
- find out information
- make choices
- cope with setbacks by trying again
- insist on being treated with respect.

Citizenship/ASDAN Award Scheme (module 1)

The ways in which self-advocacy is fostered become part of the whole ethos of the school. At Piper Hill, for instance, staff are aware of equal opportunities through

TERMLY PLANNING SHEET				
Term Summer	**Year** 1998	**Curriculum Area** PSE	**Class** KS4 Groups 3 & 4	**N.C. Year** 10 & 11

SOURCE: Piper Hill PSE Curriculum
ASDAN Award Scheme

AIMS: 1. To write up last term's completed ASDAN challenges
2. To complete section of work on Road Traffic Safety
3. To complete section of work on Personal Safety and ASDAN challenge
3. To work with individual pupil and her carer on a specific Sex Education programme

SPECIFIC TEACHING POINTS/OBJECTIVES

Traffic Safety   – to practise road safety skills and to learn where to play and where to cross the road; wearing correct clothing

Personal Safety – to make sensible choices, saying yes or no and practise assertiveness to understand 'stranger danger'

General Safety – to know who will help us – asking for help keeping safe at home and near water

ASDAN   – Family/Home Personal Autonomy Challenge

ACTIVITIES/RESOURCES USED

LDA (1994) Protection Pack – yes/no cards, stories, Makaton sheets
Drama and role play using Protection Pack stories
Role play assertiveness games and class discussions
Pat Mason – Police Schools Liaison Officer – Well Safe (Suzy Lampugh Trust, 1995)
Police video on road safety, bright safe clothing and work on keeping safe in other situations
With school nurse on specific Sex Education programme – see separate sheet

CROSS-CURRICULAR LINKS:

English – Speaking and Listening

Figure 10.1 ASDAN Award Scheme planning sheet

training, and are prepared to challenge one another or the system if appropriate. Pupils are actively encouraged to help one another – for example, a FE pupil regularly cooks with a younger class. They are helped to select their own dinner, and wherever possible encouraged to act independently – for instance, travelling to college placements by bus.

Pupils are constantly helped to reach small targets so that they may enjoy the feeling of success. Our pupils do an action plan and review for ASDAN Award Scheme credits (see Figure 10.1; also Chapter 11) and are encouraged to plan and improve their own learning through this scheme. Rites of passage are celebrated: thus on transition from KS3 to KS4 and KS4 to FE each pupil receives a certificate.

Small achievements and pupils' interests are shared and celebrated at assemblies – for example, at an assembly focusing on 'our hobbies' a pupil gave a talk about her membership of the Girl Guides. Pupils also enjoy contributing to the school newsletter.

Class rules for behaviour are drawn up by the pupils themselves. They help to look after their classroom and their own property. We use drama in the curriculum to encourage pupils to explore other roles, to develop confidence, their own learning and the ability to solve problems. They are taught about decision making and they help to run events at school, for instance through the School Council – a whole school project at Piper Hill – where one pupil is elected from each tutor group to be a representative. The Council runs as a proper business meeting with elected members such as Chairperson and Treasurer. (The module descriptions in Figure 10.2 describes part of the setting up of the Council and how it linked with the city wide Manchester Schools' Council.) The Council meets about every half term and helps to plan school events and makes decisions, such as on the running of the school Youth Club. The Council has also planned and run an end-of-term disco, and the pupil representatives helped to set up and run the lunchtime club for the Healthy School Award (see below).

Pupils are encouraged to evaluate their year's work in writing if possible and by speaking at their Annual Review. Parents are consulted and involved in decision making for their own children as well as on wider issues such as helping to develop the school grounds.

Skills development through the Healthy School Award (module 2)

When Piper Hill entered the Healthy School Award in 1997, one of our aims was to improve the self-advocacy skills of our pupils, particularly the older pupils.

Initially a working party was formed to plan our work; this consisted of two pupils, two non-teaching members of staff, a senior manager, the school nurse and a parent governor. We met each month and focused on developing our lunchtime activities, the Youth Club and sport in the community (basketball and gymnastics). We also chose and set up health weeks in school, such as the Food Awareness Week.

ASDAN Module Title	The School Council (2)	Towards Independence Committees/User Groups
Curriculum Area	**Citizenship**	

Description of Module

The students will have experience of working as a group (committee) on a task (jigsaw, game) without the help of adults, who will be observers only.
Students will form a committee/council and carry out two tasks:

1. The students share in the discussion to decide how to talk with the pupils in KSs 3 & 4 about the formation of the School Council. They will demonstrate that they understand the task of being in the group that talks to the pupils.

2. Share in the organisation of a visit to Manchester Town Hall showing understanding of the sequence of tasks to be done.

They will share in the discussion as members of the committee, contributing, answering questions and taking part in a vote.
With support they will be able to talk about the roles of the members of the group.

Outcomes

In successfully completing the module students will have – with verbal support:

1. Co-operated well in a group task, showing commitment, initiative, support and appropriate language/gesture.

2. Taken part in group discussion, showing understanding of the tasks being undertaken.

3. Know who, within the group is doing a particular job.

4. Taken part in a vote.

5. Go with the committee to explain about the formation of the School Council to the pupils in KSs 3 & 4.

Module Specification	Assessment Procedures
Students will have fulfilled the above criteria and the outcomes will have been demonstrated	Staff dated records The Minute Book Video and photographs

Evidence to Support Outcomes

Video of the group work

The Minute Book

The first meeting of the School Council

Photographs of the Committee at work

Figure 10.2 Work involved in setting up the school council

The idea of the Keeping Healthy Lunchtime Club was suggested and developed at our Healthy School meetings, and the work for this was mainly carried out by senior pupils with the help of Christine, our school nurse, and Jenny, a GNVQ student. The pupils organised a programme of events, signed up a group of pupils who wanted to attend the club, and organised a vote to choose a popular name for their Keeping Healthy Lunchtime Club. The Body Beautiful Club, as it became, went on to plan activities for the summer term 1998, starting with badge making and including fruit tasting, line dancing, hand and foot massage, facials and keep fit. The activities of the Body Beautiful Club link with the PE (keep fit, line dancing, ball skills), Sensory, and Food Technology (food tasting) curriculum at school and help pupils to develop confidence, independence and the ability to make choices (in choosing activities, getting themselves to the club and mixing with friends outside their peer group). Some of these activities are linked to pupils' Individual Targets for Learning formulated by class tutors, such as 'I can look after my own clothes' or 'I can work with my friends in a group'.

The pupils were presented with the Silver Award in the Healthy School Award in April 1998 at an award ceremony for schools, where displays of their work were presented. Later, we took part in and gained the Gold Award. Through all the work generated by their activities the pupils have increased their communication skills, gained knowledge of running a group, developed their ideas and felt justifiably proud of their achievements.

The work and achievements of the pupils have also given the teaching staff an impetus to find other ways of developing pupils' self-advocacy skills at school.

Chapter 11

Independence and Leisure

Working towards independence

Helping pupils to be as independent as possible at home, in school and in the wider community is ongoing, and starts from an early age. As pupils progress through school they should follow a programme of learning based on needs and abilities and on close cooperation between home and school.

The work in Key Stage 4 is based on the ASDAN Award Scheme 'Transition Challenge'. In the FE Department the emphasis of the curriculum is on pupil independence and pupils work towards the ASDAN Award 'Towards Independence'.

Independence skills/ASDAN Award Scheme (module 1)

The Award Scheme Development and Accreditation Network (ASDAN), based at the University of the West of England in Bristol, offers a number of programmes for students of all abilities. The scheme started in the 1980s, and currently has over 2,000 registered centres.

ASDAN was established by a group of teachers and trainers to promote good practice in relation to personal skills development.

The Transition Challenge (Figures 11.1, 11.2, 11.3) is a new ASDAN entry level programme, which provides a context for the accreditation of achievement by students aged 14–16 (and beyond) with complex and/or severe (SLD) learning disabilities. The programme provides a framework of activities for developing and accrediting independent living and personal skills through areas of activity relating to statutory programmes of study for Key Stage 4 National Curriculum subjects. The activities also contribute to the skills of adult living, as recommended by the Dearing Report (Dearing, 1996).

After initial training the scheme was introduced at Piper Hill by a KS 4 teacher in the spring of 1997, and we began the process of working towards moderation by a regional coordinator. To date, ASDAN work at Piper Hill has involved two teacher training sessions; setting up of pupil record books; setting up of a Central Development Plan File; meeting parents/carers to explain the scheme; coordinating the writing of the subject modules (see example at Figure 11.4); attending regional meetings (three times a year); developing pupils' assessment and recording work; holding meetings for teaching staff on work in hand; and training and assisting non-teaching staff to implement the scheme.

TRANSITION CHALLENGE
(Working Towards Independence)

ASDAN
AWARD
SCHEME

An Entry level programme for young people aged 14–16 (and beyond) with severe and complex learning difficulties

The Transition Challenge (Working Towards Independence) provides a context for the accreditation of achievement by students with complex, severe, profound or multiple learning difficulties. The programme is learner-centred and offers opportunities for a negotiated, modular, and activity-based curriculum.

The programme comprises five modules, incorporating a range of activities which can be undertaken with as much support as necessary. Achievement is recorded across the range of statutory programmes for Key Stage 4 National Curriculum subjects, complemented by activities contributing to the skills of adult living, as recommended by the Dearing Review of 14–19 provision.

Module titles are taken from the Transition Planning Section (6.42–6.60) of the Code of Practice for the Assessment of Special Education Needs. Students undertaking the Transition Challenge will need to complete eight out of twelve possible areas of activity within each of the five modules. These areas of activity focus on National Curriculum subjects and issues recommended by the Dearing Report (Dearing, 1996).

TRANSITION CHALLENGE MODULES:				
1. INDEPENDENT LIVING SKILLS	2. SELF ADVOCACY	3. POSITIVE SELF-IMAGE	4. PERSONAL DEVELOPMENT	5. PERSONAL AUTONOMY

AREAS OF ACTIVITY		
• English	• Mathematics	• Science
• Design and Technology	• Modern Foreign Language	• Information Technology
• Religious Education	• Recreation	• Sport and Leisure
• Family/Home	• Community	• Vocational Education

The Transition Challenge is presented in an A4 Student Record Book and the Guidance and Resources for Tutors incorporates Activity Resources, with and without Rebus (Widgit) symbols. These resources are optional and offer an example of how the areas of activity could be broken down into smaller steps.

The Transition Challenge offers progression into the ASDAN Towards Independence programme.

For an information pack please contact:
☎ ASDAN Central Office, 27 Redland Hill, Bristol BS6 6UX Tel: 0117 923 9843

Figure 11.1 The ASDAN Transition Challenge outlined (reproduced with permission from ASDAN)

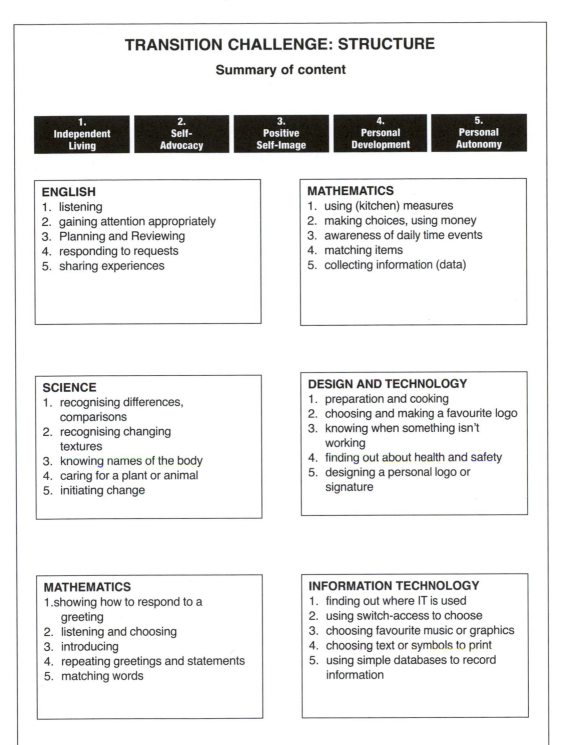

Figure 11.2 The ASDAN Transition Challenge structure (reproduced with permission from ASDAN)

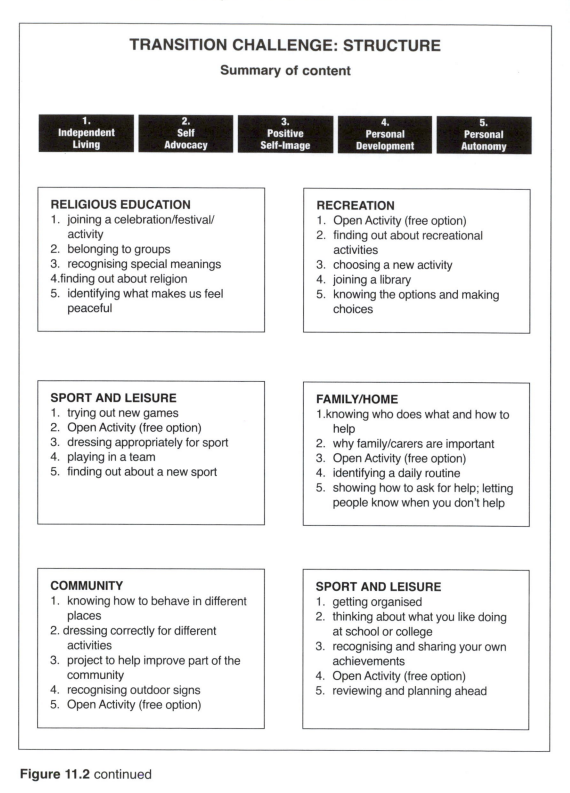

TRANSITION CHALLENGE: STRUCTURE
Summary of content

1. Independent Living	2. Self Advocacy	3. Positive Self-Image	4. Personal Development	5. Personal Autonomy

RELIGIOUS EDUCATION
1. joining a celebration/festival/ activity
2. belonging to groups
3. recognising special meanings
4. finding out about religion
5. identifying what makes us feel peaceful

RECREATION
1. Open Activity (free option)
2. finding out about recreational activities
3. choosing a new activity
4. joining a library
5. knowing the options and making choices

SPORT AND LEISURE
1. trying out new games
2. Open Activity (free option)
3. dressing appropriately for sport
4. playing in a team
5. finding out about a new sport

FAMILY/HOME
1. knowing who does what and how to help
2. why family/carers are important
3. Open Activity (free option)
4. identifying a daily routine
5. showing how to ask for help; letting people know when you don't help

COMMUNITY
1. knowing how to behave in different places
2. dressing correctly for different activities
3. project to help improve part of the community
4. recognising outdoor signs
5. Open Activity (free option)

SPORT AND LEISURE
1. getting organised
2. thinking about what you like doing at school or college
3. recognising and sharing your own achievements
4. Open Activity (free option)
5. reviewing and planning ahead

Figure 11.2 continued

ASDAN TRANSITION CHALLENGE
KS4–PSE

Year 1 – Autumn Term	Spring Term	Summer Term
Family/Home – Independent Living Skills Show you know who does what jobs in your family. Suggest three ways to help.	**Family/Home – Self-Advocacy** Say why different family members are important to you. Choose appropriate birthday presents for them.	**Family/Home – Personal Autonomy** Show you know how to ask for help when you need it. Show how to let others know when you don't need help.

Year 2 – Autumn Term	Spring Term	Summer Term
Family/Home and Science – Positive Self-Image Open activity which you and your family/carer can choose. Take part in personal hygiene activities. Show you know the names of different body parts. Understand that it can be inappropriate to touch or be touched in particular places.	**Family/Home – Personal Development** Choose a daily routine with your family. Show you understand what you have to do and when.	**Family/Home** In the sixth term the pupils' work is assembled for final accreditation.

Figure 11.3 ASDAN Transition Challenge timetable (see Figure 4.4 for how this timetable is used for work on module 2 of Family Life Education)

PIPER HILL MATHEMATICS MODULE

MODULE NUMBER: MEASUREMENT

MODULE TITLE: USING KITCHEN SCALES

ASDAN: TRANSITION CHALLENGE – INDEPENDENT SKILLS

MODULE DESCRIPTION

Pupils will complete a series of activities involving comparing the weight of two objects to determine which is the heavier/lighter. They will use non-standard units of measure practically in Food Technology lessons (cupfuls and spoonfuls) and standard units of measure (grams) using kitchen scales. They will follow recipes using non-standard measures and standard measures and keep a record of what they have made, in the form of a recipe book, over a period of at least one term. Pupils will make drinks at breaktime filling cups from a jug (cupfuls and jugfuls) to help develop understanding of capacity.

ASSESSMENT PROCEDURES

Staff dated records. Photographs of pupils weighing. The pupil recipe book .Photographs of pupil making drinks. Worksheets Booklets

MODULE SPECIFICATION

Outcomes 1–4 to be demonstrated. For some pupils it will also be appropriate for outcome 5 to be demonstrated.

OUTCOMES

In successfully completing this unit, pupils show they can:

1. make drinks for their friends at breaktime including mixing water and juice in a jug and pouring juice into cups,

2. use scales to compare the weight of two objects and which is heavier/lighter,

3. use spoonfuls and cupfuls as units of measure in Food Technology,

4. use kitchen scales to weigh ingredients for a recipe,

5. follow a recipe and use kitchen scales accurately to weigh ingredients.

National Curriculum AT3, Level 1/2

Figure 11.4 Example of subject module for the ASDAN Transition Challenge

We like the scheme at Piper Hill because:

- it is learner-centred
- it offers a framework of negotiated activities
- it enriches our curriculum
- it offers small steps to achievement
- it promotes and records achievements
- it is nationally recognised external accreditation
- it develops key skills
- it provides progression to the 'Towards Independence' challenge and Bronze Award studied in FE.

Leisure activities (module 2)

Leisure forms a large part of our pupils' lives, and their participation in a wide range of activities enriches their experience of the world. Leisure activities can be broken down into the areas of sports and games, creative arts, and leisure at home. Through participation in all of these activities, people with SLD and PMLD can interact more fully with their environment.

The list of activities suggested here includes examples only and is not exhaustive. Schools need to compile their own comprehensive and up-to-date list of resources to help staff, parents and carers organise a broad leisure and independence programme. This would include addresses and telephone numbers of local venues where activities can be pursued. For example:

- Sports and games: leisure centres, swimming pools, bowling alleys, roller/ice skating, athletics facilities, riding stables, sailing/water sports centre, walking association, cycling association, fitness centre, exercise/dance studio, adventure playgrounds, football clubs/grounds;
- Creative arts: art galleries, craft centres, museums, theatres, libraries, cinemas, opera house, dance groups, funfairs, concert halls;
- Leisure at home: Gateway club, Guide and Scout groups, Woodwork groups, Boys Brigade, leisure clubs, parks, farms, zoos, stately homes, cafes, restaurants.

Some general addresses are given at the end of this chapter.

The checklists of achievements under these headings, which follow, indicate the range of activities which pupils can be encouraged to pursue.

Sports and games

☐ I can play games with my friends, e.g. ludo, snakes and ladders, bingo, lotto, dominoes, playing cards, darts, snooker, billiards, table tennis, table football, cooperative games, 'parachute' games (circle games to develop group skills – see Masheder, 1989), indoor rounders, skittles, volley ball and boccia (see p108 for address)..

☐ I can use facilities in my community, e.g. local leisure centres, swimming pool, (swimming for disabled), sauna, gymnasium facilities and Gym Club, trampolining, badminton.

☐ I can take part in games and outdoor pursuits, e.g. rounders, cricket, football, canoeing, sailing, walking, orienteering (wheelchair friendly), cycling, aerobics, popmobility.

☐ I can organise a visit to a spectator sport, e.g. football, basket ball, ice hockey.

Creative arts

☐ I enjoy using creative materials, e.g. painting, collage, puppets, fabrics, design crafts, papier mâché, clay modelling, sewing/embroidery.

☐ I can take part in drama activities, e.g. drama group, charades.

☐ I can use facilities in my community, e.g. art galleries, craft galleries, museums, libraries, theatres, cinemas.

☐ I enjoy listening to and making music, e.g. keyboard, use of stereo/cassette/CD system, Karaoke, music and movement activities.

☐ I enjoy dancing, e.g. wheelchair dancing, disco, old time dancing, folk dancing, line dancing

Leisure at home

☐ I enjoy hobbies at home, e.g. TV/radio, computer games, reading magazines/newspapers, jigsaws, cookery, gardening, beauty therapy and make-up.

☐ I enjoy days out and holidays, e.g. parks, stately homes, canal trips, zoos, farms, cafés and restaurants.

☐ I can be a member of an organised group, e.g. Guides, Scouts, Boys Brigade, leisure clubs – Gateway, Gym Club, school Youth Club.

Resources and useful addresses

An information pack which provides an excellent basis for planning pupils' independence and leisure activities at school – and for parents and carers or those running play schemes – is MENCAP's *Leisure for People with Profound and Multiple Disabilities* (Hogg, 1991). As well as outlining general strategy for people with learning disabilities, the pack contains descriptions of specific leisure activities with an accompanying video tape. The pack is divided into sections including *Getting Started*, and six booklets of leisure activities cover *Sports, Games and Adaptations, Creative Arts, Therapies, Sensory Environments, Planning Workshops* and *Developing Leisure Plans*.

A group which acts as a bridge into the community, giving individuals and groups confidence to participate in community activities, is Gateway (The National Federation of Gateway Clubs, Mencap National Centre, 117-123 Golden Lane, London EC1Y 0RT. Tel: 0171 454 0454). Some gateway clubs take their members rambling, rock climbing, horse riding, canoeing and on holiday. Others concentrate on team sports, drama or musical activities.

Two suppliers of toys are ROMPA (Goyt Side Road, Chesterfield, Derbyshire SK40 2PH), which will advise on soft play activities and equipment for a multi-sensory area, and Toys for the Handicapped (76 Barracks Road, Sandy Lane Industrial Estate, Stourport-on-Severn, Worcestershire DY13 9QB).

Other useful contacts are:

Arts Council of England, 14 Great Peter Street, London SW1P 3NQ (produces a free Arts and Disability Directory).

ASDAN Central Office, 27 Redland Hill, Bristol BS6 6UX. Tel: 01179 239843.

Boccia, the sport for all, is played at every level from the school playground to the Paralympic games. It can be played at school, sports clubs, locally and nationally. The TOP SportSability programme will lead to wider availability of boccia eqipment and information about how to play the game. For further information about the game, contact the British Boccia Federation, c/o 11 Churchill Park, Colwick, Nottinghampshire NG4 2 HF. Tel: 0115 941 8418.

Disabled Living Foundation Music Advisory Service, 380-384 Harrow Road, London W9 2HU. Tel: 0171 289 6111.

Disability Sport England, National Junior Sports Officer, NGB Disabilities Development Project Officer, 13 Brunswick Place, London N1 6DX. Tel: 0171 490 4919 – organise junior events including SportSability games (see Boccia).

RADAR, 12 City Forum, 250 City Road, London EC1V 8AF (provides information on sports centres and holidays for people with disabilities).

REMAP (Technical Equipment for Disabled People) 'Hazeldene', Ightham, Sevenoaks, Kent TN15 9AD. Tel: 01732 883818.

Riding for the Disabled Association (RDA), RDA Headquarters, Avenue D, National Agricultural Centre, Stoneleigh Park, Warwickshire CV8 2LY. Tel: 01203 696510.

Appendix

Training for Sex Education at Piper Hill

Sex education questionnaire

As outlined in Chapter 1, the process of developing our PSE curriculum began when we invited our teachers and nursery nurses to complete a questionnaire about sex education. The questionnaire is shown in Figure A.1. When the results of the questionnaire were analysed (Figure A.2), these identified a range of areas in which it was realised we needed to develop and trial detailed curricula and work plans.

Training for governors

To forward our plans, our governors were invited to attend a sex education training session. The programme arranged for them is shown in Figure A.3. The results of the brainstorming session are shown in Figure A.4 and those of the 'ordering statements' exercise in Figure A.5.

Training for staff

The day training programme for staff is shown in Figure A.6, with notes for group leaders (Figure A.7) and resulting ideas (Figure A.8). The building blocks exercise is shown graphically in Figure A.9, and text of the legislation quiz is given in Figure A.10. (Legislation tends to change from time to time, and PSE coordinators need to keep themselves up to date with such issues.) The Evaluation sheet is shown in Figure A.11 and responses to our one-day programme given on 24 May 1996 are shown in Figure A.12.

Questionnaire for Teachers and Nursery Nurses about Sex Education and Health Education at Piper Hill School

Name (Teacher of Class) .... Date: ....

Age Group: ....

Please could you enclose a copy of your Summer '96 and Autumn '96 plans for Sex and Health Education

1. List the areas you would like to cover in Sex and Health Education

2. Which books and teaching materials do you use?

3. Have you used any videos?

4. How do you teach the subject, e.g., one-to-one, in mixed groups, in single sex groups? Where do you work?

5. Who in your team is involved in Sex/Health Education work?

6. In which areas of Sex Education would you like training?

7. How confident do you feel in meeting pupils' needs for Sex Education?

Please return to Linda Otten by 10th October
Thank you.

Figure A.1 Questionnaire for staff

Questionnaire for Teachers, Nursery Nurses and Support Workers about Sex and Health Education at Piper Hill School

Questionnaire Results

Areas we would like to cover

Subject	Number
puberty and body changes (physical and emotional)	3
how the body works	2
relationships	4
sex – physical aspects	2
masturbation	4
correct vocabulary	2
personal hygiene	3
menstruation	2
stranger danger	1
first aid	1
toilet training	1
how to deal with sexual approaches from older pupils	3
appropriate work for PMLD students	1

Areas in which we would like training

all	8
menstruation	1
masturbation	2
HIV/AIDS	1
safe sex	1
sexual relationships	2
contraception	1
sexuality	1
issues in Secondary education	3
PMLD students and sexuality	2
sexual approaches from older pupils	1
vocabulary	1
mechanics of reproduction	1
functions of certain body parts	1

Figure A.2 Sex Education questionnaire – results

Piper Hill High School: Development of Sex Education – Training Session for Governors

Thursday 16th November, 4.30 – 5.30 p.m.

PROGRAMME

4.30   **Introductions** followed by **How did we get our own sex education?**

Work in pairs. The facilitator co-ordinates feedback, drawing out positive examples/experiences.

4.40   **Where, when, what and how do young people at Piper Hill currently get their sex education?**

A brainstorm exercise (either in whole group or two small groups).

4.50   **Feedback:** the facilitator processes – drawing out the importance of what we are doing and why we are doing it.

4.55   **What do we mean by 'sex education'?**

An 'ordering statements' exercise to explore the issues. This is done in small groups.

5.10   **Feedback:** a whole group discussion/comments.

5.15   **Current legislation**

A quiz to highlight the main requirements of current legislation.

5.25   The co-ordinator gives an update on what's happened so far.

5.30   Close

Figure A.3 Initial training session for governors led by Cath Fletcher, a Senior Health Promotion Officer, and the PSE coordinater

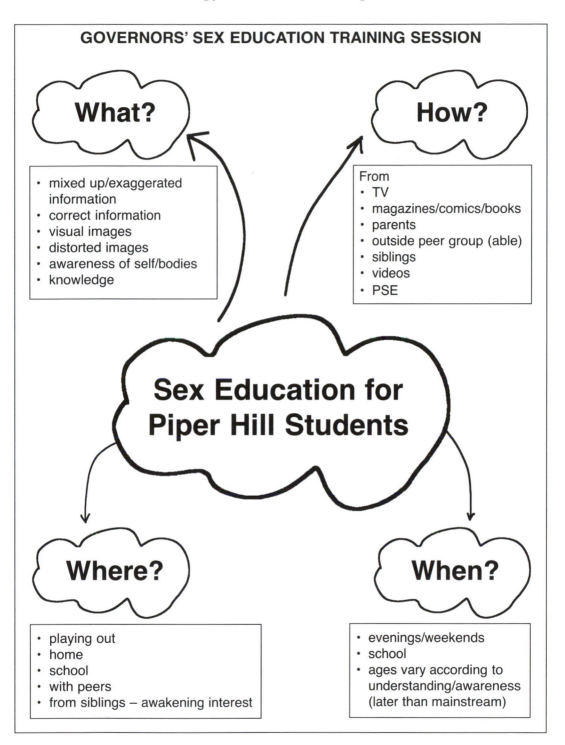

Figure A.4 How do young people at Piper Hill currently get sex education?

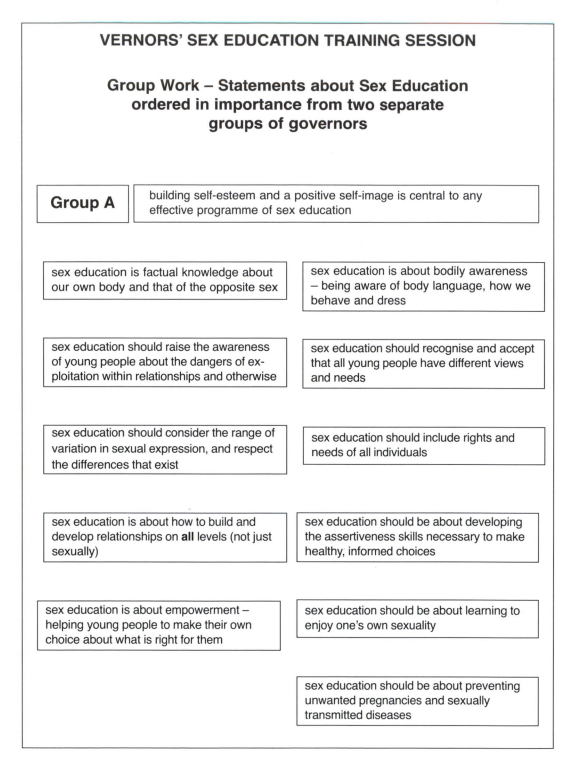

Figure A.5 What do we mean by 'sex education'?

Group B

sex education is about empowerment – helping young people to make their own choice about what is right for them	sex education is about how to build and develop relationships on **all** levels (not just sexually)
Sex education is factual knowledge about our own body and that of the opposite sex	building self-esteem and a positive self-image is central to any effective programme of sex education
Sex education should help young people to take responsibility for their sexual behaviour	sex education should be about learning to enjoy one's own sexuality
sex education should be about preventing unwanted pregnancies and sexually transmitted diseases	sex education should recognise and accept that all young people have different views and needs
sex education should raise the awareness of young people about the dangers of ex-ploitation within relationships and otherwise	sex education should include rights and needs of all individuals

Figure A.5 continued

Programme for Sex Education Training Day
for all Staff
Piper Hill High School

Main facilitator: Linda Otten

Group facilitators: Janet Ashton, Christine Galligan, Tracey Dixon, Lesley Doran, Judy Mapplebeck, Jane Lilleyman, Linda Jones.

Morning session led by Linda Otten:

9.00 a.m.   **Welcome and Introduction** (staff should sit in groups of six or eight).

9.05 a.m.   **Ground Rules.** Small group work: the group decides the rules and writes them down on paper.

9.20 a.m.   **Love Hearts game.** Small group work: everyone takes a Love Heart sweet and links the message on it to an aspect of sex education.

9.30 a.m.   **What is Sex Education?** Small group work: brainstorming – the leader writes down the ideas, which are discussed and written on ten bricks (to be mounted on the wall).

9.55 a.m.   **Legislation Quiz.** Small group work: answering the questions.

10.00 a.m.   **Answers to quiz**, presented by Linda Otten.

10.15 a.m.   **Break**

10.30 a.m.   1. **Puppet Workshop**. Elizabeth Gamlin presents her Baby Sam, puppetry work for use with senior students.

                 2. **Sex Education in School.** Examples of components of a school sex education programme are presented and discussed, with Judy Mapplebeck, Jane Lilleyman, and Linda Otten.

12.00 noon   **Lunch**

Figure A.6 Training for staff

Afternoon session led by Cath Fletcher, Senior Health Promotion Officer:

12.45 pm **Lucky Dip activity.** Small group work: participants take an item from the bag and say how they think it links to Sex Education.

1.00 p.m. Cath Fletcher takes feedback from session and discusses Sex Education

1.15 p.m **When, Where, What and How do the young people with whom we work get their Sex Education?** Small group work brainstorming on flip-charts.

1.30 p.m. Cath Fletcher draws out main points we have learnt.

1.35 p.m. Two groups

1. **Work covered so far in school.** Linda Otten, with Janet Ashton, Linda Jones and Christine Galligan.

2. **Collage exercise.** Pairs work: using scrap materials such as fur, plastic balls, cardboard tubes, etc. participants construct sexual body parts to help build up knowledge of anatomy and confidence about discussing Sex Education; with Cath Fletcher.

2.10 p.m. Tea/coffee to be taken as the two groups swap over.

2.45 p.m. **Evaluation Forms.** These to be completed by participants.

2.55 p.m. **Cartoon exercise.** Small group work: each group has an enlarged version of a cartoon from a magazine or newspaper and thinks up a caption to sum up the day.

3.00 p.m. **Close.**

Figure A.6 Training for staff

Ground rules

Ask for ideas from the group. Write all ideas down on paper provided Group leader should keep her own list for prompts. For example: confidentiality; space to speak, for self and others; respect for others; trying not to make assumptions; no undue pressure to speak or disclose anything we don't want to. Explain that the subject and some issues can be sensitive, so it is important to agree to develop a supportive atmosphere in which to work.

Love Hearts game

The messages on the Love Heart sweets are currently appropriate for this purpose. There may be time for more than one go each.

What is Sex Education? (see Figure A.10)

Write down all the ideas on a large list and discuss them. Then, in the group, choose the ten which are felt to be most important and write them on bricks' to go on the wall (see Figure A.5).

Legislation quiz

This should take about five minutes, working in pairs or on their own. Do not make it seem like a test – no one will have to give their score. The answers are:

1. True for primary schools, but for secondary schools it is a legal requirement to provide a separate programme of Sex Education.

2. True. Information on the policy must be made available to parents who request it. Many schools use the school brochure to do this.

3. True, but children cannot be withdrawn from those aspects covered in the National Curriculum.

4. True, but there is no definition of the term 'family' or 'value'.

5. True.

6. True. Teachers can give information but one-to-one advice should be left to the appropriate professionals, i.e. the school nurse.

Figure A.7 Notes for group leaders

Puppet workshop
Elizabeth Gamlin's presentation uses shadow puppets to inform pupils about conception, contraception and some of the emotional aspects of sexuality. The workshop is very much tailored to meet the needs and developmental stage of the pupils. Elizabeth Gamlin has recently moved from Manchester to Oxfordshire and her address is given in the Bibliography and Resource List. She is willing to travel.

Sex Education in school
There are good examples in On the Agenda (Scott et al, 1994), such as assertive (saying no); personal hygiene for older students; game to teach public/private. You will need to promote discussion of your completed Sex Education programme.

Lucky Dip activity
Each member of the group takes an item (no looking). The bag should contain items such as shaving cream, a condom, tampons, alcohol, wedding confetti, an injecting needle (in a case), contraceptive pills and a deodorant. This exercise is to explore the wider range if issues and attitudes connected with sex education and to encourage staff to feel at ease talking about the subject.

When, where, what and how ... ?
Brainstorm and write up on a flip chart how participants think the students at school currently get their sex education.

Large group sessions
There should be about 35 minutes to spend in each group.

Evaluation forms
Evaluation is an important process and this time is put aside to ensure that the forms are completed.

Figure A.7 continued

Issues to consider when working with groups of pupils

Confidentiality is important (but see also Chapter 3). You will need to plan your group: is it to be single sex, mixed sex, or an age group? The environment is important: it needs to be somewhere where the group and the leader feel relaxed.

Considerations when working with pupils or other staff members

A competent leader is crucial: the leader should be confident and able to explore difficult issues. Everyone should be accorded the right to express themselves; there should be no put-downs. Respect should be shown for what people say; all participants should be encouraged to listen to show that they value what is being said. Leaders should be prepared to change the plan: this is another way of showing that you value what is being said. Allow people to initiate discussion. Seek the involvement of parents in the planning stage; show respect for different cultures and religious values; and accept a person's choice of language and body language.

What is Sex Education?

It is factual knowledge and body awareness of one's own body and the body of the opposite sex – at an appropriate level. It is an awareness of the effect of body language and how you dress. It is learning to be in control: of owning your own body and the rights over your own body. Assertiveness and self-respect are important qualities to develop. Individuals have a right to say no, a right to choose within socially and morally acceptable boundaries appropriate to the individual. It involves an awareness and acceptance that different people have different views and needs. It is learning about different types of relationships, and how to make relationships on all levels, not just sexually. The fostering of self-esteem and self-worth is an important part of the Sex Education programme. It deals also with vulnerability ('stranger danger') and appropriate behaviour. Sex Education is education for life; it is the whole approach to relationships. It is an awareness of differences between men and women, understanding our own sexuality; wanting to be liked and accepted by others; to be more confident in ourselves; portraying different facets of ourselves. It is that each pupil would have the knowledge and understanding to make informed and safe choices regarding their sexuality, emotions and relationships. It is learning about the biological and moral progression of life.

Figure A.8 General notes – issues which were identified on the training day

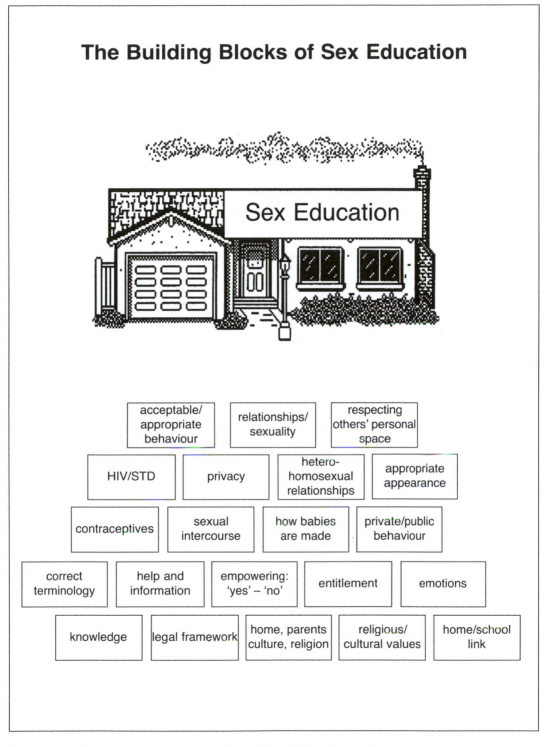

The Building Blocks of Sex Education

Sex Education

| acceptable/ appropriate behaviour | relationships/ sexuality | respecting others' personal space |

| HIV/STD | privacy | hetero- homosexual relationships | appropriate appearance |

| contraceptives | sexual intercourse | how babies are made | private/public behaviour |

| correct terminology | help and information | empowering: 'yes' – 'no' | entitlement | emotions |

| knowledge | legal framework | home, parents culture, religion | religious/ cultural values | home/school link |

Figure A.9 Staff training group exercise: What is Sex Education?

Sex Education Legislation and Guidance
– a quiz

1. Schools are being encouraged to include sex education in the curriculum.

   True ☐

   False ☐

2. Schools have a legal duty to inform parents of their policy on sex education.

   True ☐

   False ☐

3. Parents have a legal right to withdraw their children from sex education.

   True ☐

   False ☐

4. Sex education must encourage pupils to have due regard to moral considerations and the value of family life.

   True ☐

   False ☐

5. There is no legislation which prohibits talking about specific sensitive issues in sex education classes.

   True ☐

   False ☐

6. Particular care must be exercised when giving advice to pupils on a one-to-one basis.

   True ☐

   False ☐

Figure A.10 Staff training group: Legislation Quiz

Evaluation

Date: ....….. Course Title: ....

1. What did you enjoy about the training?

_____

_____

2. What did you dislike about the training?

_____

_____

3. If you had one thing to say to the organisers, what would it be?

_____

_____

4. Other suggestions

_____

_____

5. What further training do you feel you need?

_____

_____

Figure A.11 Sex Education training session – evaluation form

Piper Hill Sex Education Training Day

EVALUATION

Number of participants

50 (a.m.), 36 (p.m.), including teachers, nursery nurses, special school support workers, physiotherapists, speech therapist and lunchtime organisers.

Organisers

Christine Galligan (School Nurse), Linda Otten (PSE Co-ordinator), Jenny Andrews (Headteacher), Linda Jones (Deputy Headteacher), Janet Ashton (Teacher), Jane Lilleyman (Teacher), Judy Mapplebeck (Teacher), Tracey Dixon (Nursery Nurse), Lesley Doran (Special School Support Worker), Cath Fletcher (Senior Health Promotion Officer), Elizabeth Gamlin (Puppeteer)

1. What did you enjoy about the training?

Group discussions (5)
Working with different people
Cath Fletcher's Workshop
Range of activities (2)
Informal relaxed atmosphere
Surprise element
Love Hearts game

Puppet Workshop (12)
Talking openly with colleagues
Good organisation
Practical work
Having fun with colleagues (3)
Learning – feeling more confident and
    comfortable
Interesting

2. What did you dislike about the training?

Collage work
Love Hearts game (7)
Too rushed at times (5)
Lucky Dip exercise

Make anatomy modelling
Being a Puppeteer (2)
Time was too short
Long day

Figure A.12 Sex Education training session – responses to evaluation form (figures in brackets show where more than one participant gave a similar answer)

3. If you had one thing to say to the organisers, what would it be?

Thank you (5)
Good work – I enjoyed it
Thought provoking
Too much to do on one day
Interesting
Comfortable sessions
Too rigid time-wise
Need two days
More time on one subject
More time for relaxation

Well organised (5)
Good day – unexpectedly
Plenty to do
Well planned
Excellent day
Keep up the good work – we need more!
Useful points generated – some need developing
Facts and information sheet to read at our leisure

4. Other Suggestions

More time needed, too rushed
More of these days
Well done!
Interesting day – non-threatening and enlightening

Write up comments, group work, games ideas
More information and training on a smaller scale
More discussions on different issues
Mention different religions and views on contraception

5. What further training do you feel you need?

Ongoing needs
Show activities to rest of staff
Sex Education issues related to other cultures
Looking at more resources and age appropriateness

Information on wheelchair users and the sex issue.
To continue discussions on materials and methods as we become a senior school.
Lots!

Figure A.12 Sex Education training session – responses to evaluation form (figures in brackets show where more than one participant gave a similar answer)

Bibliography and Resource List

Adcock, K. and Stanley, G. (1996) *Sexual Health Education and Children and Young People with Learning Disabilities, A Practical Way of Working for Professionals, Parents and Carers.* Plymouth: Bild Publications.

Adler, D. (1994) *A Picture Book of Anne Frank.* London: Macmillan Children's Books.

ASDAN (Award Scheme Development and Accreditation Network) Central Office, 27 Redland Hill, Bristol BS6 6UX.

British Institute for Mental Handicap (1996) Three booklets (revised): *Aids and People with Learning Difficulties, A Guide for Parents; Aids and People with Learning Difficulties, A guide for Staff and Carers, What You need to Know about HIV and Aids.* London: British Institute for Mental Handicap in conjunction with Brook Advisory Centres, Family Planning Association and MENCAP.

Boulton Hawker Films (1990) *Janet's Got Her Period.* Video and booklets. Hadleigh (Suffolk IP7 5BG): Boulton Hawker Films.

Brook Advisory Centre (1990) Male and female cloth models. London: Brook Publications.

Burns, S and Lamont, G (1995) *Values and Visions, A Handbook for Spiritual Development and Global Awareness.* London: Hodder and Stoughton.

Clarity Collective (1989) *Taught not Caught, Strategies for Sex Education.* Cambridge: LDA.

Clarke, S. (1992) *My Choice, My Own Choice.* Video and teaching materials. Brighton: Pavilion Publishing.

Craft, A. (1991) *Living Your Life.* Teacher's handbook and photocopiable sheets. Cambridge: LDA.

Craft, A. (1992) 'Sexuality', *Mental Handicap* Special Issue, vol. **20** (2). Clevedon: BIMH Publication.

Craft, A. and Dixon, H. (1992) *Picture yourself* (pack). Cambridge: LDA.

Craft, A. and Stewart, D. (1993) *What About Us? Sex Education for Children with Disabilities.* Home School Publication. Winchester: Sarsen Press.

Dearing (1996) Review of Qualifications – Dearing Full Report. London: Qualifications and Curriculum Authority.

Department of Education and Science (1986) 'Health Education from 5–16', *Curriculum Matters* No. 6. York: NCC.

Development Education Centre (1990) *What is a Family?* Photographs and activities. Birmingham: Selly Oak Colleges.

Dixon, H. (1992) *Chance to Choose.* Cambridge: LDA.

Downs, C. and Craft, A. (1997) *Sex in Context: Strategies and Safeguards Relating to the Sexuality of Children and Adults with Profound and Multiple Impairments.* Brighton: Pavilion Publishing.

Fraser, J. (1997) *Learning to Love* a set of simple booklets on sex: *From Child to Adult; Sex: How a Baby Starts; How a Baby is Born; Sex, Health and Infections; Contraception.* London: Brook Advisory Centre.

Gamlin, E. (1994) *Baby Sam* and *Outside/Inside* (educational puppet workshops). Barn Close, High Street, Long Wittenham, Near Abgindon, Oxon OX14 4QJ.

Gateway, The National Federation of Gateway Cluds, Mencap National Centre, 117–123 Golden Lane, London EC1Y 0RT Tel: 0171 454 0454.

Gogglebox, video series (1996) *Don't Smoke – You Make Me Choke!*; (1996) *Think Before You Drink*; (1997) *Beat the Bullies.* Bradford: Gogglebox Resources for Learning.

Groups in Learning (1995) *Drugs Education – A Practical Guide for Primary School Teachers.* Groups in Learning, 10 Charlotte Street, Cabot, Bristol BS1 5PX.

Headon (1996) *School Scenario Boards.* Manchester: Headon Productions (tel: 0161 225 7080).

Headon (1998) *Drugs Pics 2.* Manchester: Headon Productions.

Health Promotion Unit (Health Promotion Specialist Service), Mancunian Community Health NHS Trust, Manchester.

HMSO (1974) Health and Safety at Work Act. London: The Stationery Office.

HMSO (1988) Education Reform Act. London: The Stationery Office.

HMSO (1990) Food Safety Act. London: The Stationery Office.

HMSO (1994) Control of Substances Hazardous to Health Regulations. London: The Stationery Office.

HMSO (1995) Food Safety Regulations. London: The Stationery Office.

HMSO (1996) Education Act. London: The Stationery Office.

Hogg, J. (1991) *Leisure for People with Profound and Multiple Disabilities, A Resource Training Pack.* London: MENCAP.

Jagota, P. and Brown, V. (1998) *Food and Health, A Resource and information pack for Schools.* Manchester: Mancunian Health Promotion Specialist Service.

Knill, C. and Knill, M. (1998) *Body Awareness, Contact and Communication.* Cambridge: LDA.

Learning Development Aids (1989) *Picture My Feelings.* Photocopiable worksheets. Cambridge: LDA.

Learning Development Aids (1994) *Protection Pack.* Cambridge: LDA.

Manchester City Council (1988) *Aids Policy: Confidentiality.* Manchester City Council.

Manchester Advisory and Inspection Service (1997) *Pride, Parents' Role in Drugs and Safety Education.* Manchester: Manchester Advisory and Inspection Service.

Manchester City Council Education Department (1991) *Cross Curricular Themes, Health Education.* Careers and Occupational Information Centre, Sales Department WIIOI, Moorfoot, S1 4PQ.

Mancunian Community Health NHS Trust (1997) *Staff Information Booklet.* Manchester: Mancunian Health Promotion Specialist Service.

Masheder, M. (1989) *Let's Play Together.* London: Green Print.

Matterson, E. (1969) *This Little Puffin.* London: Puffin Books.

National Children's Bureau (1994) *Developing and Reviewing a School Sex Education Policy.* London: Sex Education Forum, National Children's Bureau.

National Children's Bureau (1995) *Developing Sex Education for Pupils with Learning Difficulties.* Forum Factsheet 7. London: Sex Education Forum, National Children's Bureau.

National Curriculum Council (1990) *Curriculum Guidance 5*. York: NCC.

Nesbit, E. (1994) *The Railway Children*. Paignton, Devon: Ladybird.

North West Dental Public Health Resource Centre (1997) *The 1995–1996 NHS Survey of Dental Decay of Five Year Old Children in the North West*. Wesham: North West Lancashire Health Authority.

Pavilion (1996) *Piece by Piece*. Video and guidance notes pack. Brighton: Pavilion Publishing.

Pudney, W. and Whitehouse, E. (1997) *A Volcano in My Tummy, Helping Children to Handle Anger*. Canada: New Society Publishers.

Ridgewell, J. (1997) *Working with Food in Primary Schools*. London: Ridgewell Press.

Ryan, M. (1995) *Health Related Resources for People with Learning Disabilities*. London: Health Education Authority.

Sarwar, G. (1994) *Sex Education and the Muslim Perspective*. London: The Muslim Education Trust.

School Curriculum Assessment Authority/Depatment for Education (1995) *Drug Education: Curriculum Guidance for Schools*. Norwich: HMSO.

Scott, L. and Image*in*Action Team (1994) *On the Agenda*. High Wycombe: Image*in*Action.

Scott, L. (1996) *Partnership with Parents in Sex Education*. London: Sex Education Forum, National Children's Bureau.

Scott, L., Johns, R. and Bliss, J. (1997) *Let's Do It*. High Wycombe: Image*in*Action.

Suzy Lamplugh Trust (1995) *Well Safe*. Video on keeping safe. London: Suzy Lamplugh Trust.

Books for pupils

Bennet, D. (1997) *Keeping Fit*. London: Belitha Press.

Cole, B. (1992) *The Hairy Book*. London: Little Mammoth.

Hawcock, D. (1997) *The Amazing Pull-out Pop-up Body in a Book*. London: Dorling Kindersley.

Hessel, J. (1987) *I'm Glad I Told Mum*. Alderley Edge, Cheshire: Beaver Books.

Hollins, S. (ed.) (1993–96) *Books Beyond Words*. Fourteen titles covering life events for SLD students. London: Royal College of Psychiatrists.

Pollards, K. 91997) *Feelings*. California, USA: Celestial Arts Publications.

Royston, A. (1995) *Getting Better – A Lift the Flap Body Book*. London: Frances Lincoln.

Wale, C. (1996) *Take Care* series of books: *Take Care at Home; Take Care On Your Own; Take Care Near Water; Take Care on The Road*. East Sussex: Wayland.

Index

IDS 21, 23
ASDAN (Award Scheme Development and
    Accreditation Network)
    and Advocacy 95, **96**, 97, 99
    and Family Life Education 43, **44**, **45**, 46
    and Independence and Leisure 101–106
    and Personal Hygiene 75, **76**, 83
    Transition Challenge 43, **44**, **45**, 101–106
    mentioned 4, 54
ablution 88
activities
    Advocacy **96**
    Environmental Aspects of Health Education
    92, 93
    Family Life Education 38, **39**, 40, 41, 43, 44,
    46, 47, 48, 49
    Food and Nutrition 67, 68, 70
    Health Related Exercise 58
    Personal Hygiene **77**, 79, 83, 87, 88
    Personal Safety 52, 53, 54, 55
    Sex Education 26, 27, 28, 29, 30, 31, 32, 33,
    34, 35
    Substance Use and Misuse 17, 18, 19, 20
adolescence 36
adult stage of life cycle **43**
adult to old person stage of life cycle **43**
advertisements
    and attitudes to health 92–3
    for hygiene products 83
advocacy
    as component of PSE 4, **5**
    developing self-esteem 95
    module 1 citizenship / ASDAN Award
    Scheme 95–7
    self-advocacy skills 95
    skills developed through Healthy School
    Award 97–100
aerosols 20
agencies, helping **48**, 49–50

aims and philosphy 3–4
alcohol **17**, 19, 20
animals, caring for 38, 40–41
annual review 10–11, 75, 76, 97
Art 79
assemblies 97
Attitudes to Food workshop 60, 70–73
Award Scheme Development and Accreditation
    Network see ASDAN

belongings 32–3
Birches, The 3, 7
Body Beautiful Club 57, 100
body functions, appropriate behaviour and
    language for 33–4
body parts
    cross-curricular links to module on 30, 31,
    34, 36
    module 1 of Sex Education programme 24,
    25, 26–9
    private 33
'boys only' groups 27
breakfast clubs 73
breakfast foods module **66**, 66–7

careers and personal care module 75, **76**, 87
careers curriculum 59
carers see parents and carers
Certificates in Personal Hygiene 75–6, 79, **80**,
    81
Certificates of Achievement for Food
    Technology **63**, **64**, **65**, **66**, **68**, **69**
challenging behaviour 2
changing facilities 88
child development and child care skills
    module 37, 46–50
Child Protection Guidelines 22–3
child rearing, patterns of 46–7
childhood **42**, 48

citizenship 95–7, **98**, **99**
City College, Manchester 3
clothes for food preparation, 60
communication 78
community, **103**
complex feelings 36
complex learning difficulties 101
condoms 29
confidentiality 22–3
continuity in learning 7
contraception 23–4, 29
Control of Substances Hazardous to Health
    Regulations (COSSH, 1994) **61**
coordinator, PSE 4, 5
coronary heart disease 71
creative arts 106, 107
cross-curricular links
    for Advocacy **96**
    for Environmental Aspects of Health
    Education 91,93
    for Family Life Education 38, **39**, 40, 41, 43,
    46, 47, 48, 49
    for Food and Nutrition 67
    for Health Related Exercise 57, 58
    for Independence and Leisure **103**
    for Personal Hygiene **77**, 79, 83
    for Personal Safety 54, 55
    for Sex Education 26, 27, 28, 30, 31, 32, 33,
    34, 36
    for Substance Use and Misuse 17, 18, 19
    and time available 7
cultural practices
    and Family Life Education 37, 46, 47
    and Food and Nutrition 60
    importance in PSE work 6
    and Personal Hygiene 87–9
    and Sex Education 32
curriculum plan (Years 7–11) **6**

Dearing Report 101, **102**
death **43**
defining Personal and Social Education 1–2
delivery 6
dental care 75, **76**, 83, **85**, **86**, 87
dental caries 71
Design and Technology **103**
diet 91, 92–3 *see also* Food and Nutrition
diseases
    prevention of **48**
    spread of 92
drama **39**, 97
drugs *see* Substance Use and Misuse

Education Act (1996) 1
Education Reform Act (1988) 1
emergency services 54
energy from food 57, 58
English
    and advocacy **96**
    and ASDAN Transition Challenge **103**
    and Environmental Aspects of Health
    Education 93
    and Family Life Education 37, **39**, 40, 43, 46
    and Food and Nutrition 67
    and Health Related Exercise 58
    and Personal Hygiene **77**, 79
    and Personal Safety 54
    and Sex Education 26, 30, 36
    and Substance Use and Misuse 17, 18, 19
environment, care of 94
Environmental Aspects of Health Education
    as component of PSE **5**
    curricular links 91
    module 1 a balanced healthy lifestyle 91–2
    module 2 the spread of diseases 92
    module 3 the influence of the media 92–3
    module 4 taking responsibility 93–4
equal opportunities 3, 47
evaluation
    PSE 10–12
    of staff training on sex education **116**, **120**,
    121
exercise
    and Environmental Aspects of Health
    Education 91, 92
    Health Related **5**, 57–8

FE see Further Education
family/home
    and Independence and Leisure **103**, **104**
    see also Family Life Education
Family Life Education
    as component of PSE **5**
    module 1 growing up in a family 38, **38**,
    40–42, **42–3**
    module 2 my family and my role in my
    family **38**, 43–6
    module 3 child development and child care
    37, 46–50
    termly planning sheet **39**
family members 46
feelings module 24, **25**, 35-6
    cross-curricular links to 27, 30, 33, 34
female/male differences 26–7
fitness and health module 58

Food and Nutrition/Food Technology
  Attitudes to Food workshop 60, 70–73
  as component of PSE **5**
  and Environmental Aspects of Health 91, 92
  and Food Technology curriculum 59, **59**, 91
  hygiene and safety rules 60–63
  issues and attitudes 60
  module 2 healthy eating 63, **63**
  module 3 safety in the kitchen 64, **64**
  module 4 planning and making a simple
    meal 65, **65**
  module 6 breakfast foods 66, 66–7
  module 8 food groups (vitamins) 67–8, **68**
  module 10 healthy eating **69**, 69–70
  mentioned 57, 58, 100
Food and Safety Act (1990) **61**
Food Awareness Week 97
food groups (vitamins) module 67–8, **68**
Food Hygiene and Handling course 59
Food Safety (General Food Hygiene)
    Regulations (1995) **61**
Food Safety (Northern Ireland) Order (1991)
    61
Food Safety (Temperature Control) Regulations
    (1995) **61**
food shortages and surpluses 94
Food Technology *see* Food and Nutrition /
    Food Technology
fruit 67
Further Education (FE)
  careers and personal care module 75, 87
  curriculum 3, **8–9**, 91, 94
  sandwich business 59
  and Sex Education 24

games 106–7
Gamlin, Elizabeth 78, **116**
gardening 73
Gateway 107
gay men 24
Geography 37, 47
'girls only' groups 27
glue sniffing 20
governors
  and PSE co-ordinator 5
  and sex education 4, 24, 109, **112**, **113**,
    114
groups
  establishing group feeling 35
  group building activities 51–2
growing from young to old 41–2, **42–3**

HIV 21, 23
hand washing, 79, 83
health and safety, food 60–63
Health and Safety at Work Act (1974) **61**
Health Promotion Specialist Service 4
Health Related Exercise
  as component of PSE **5**
  cross-curricular links 57
  module 1 fitness and health 58
health weeks 73, 97
healthy eating modules 63, **63**, **69**, 69-70
  cross-curricular links to 57, 91
Healthy School Award 71, 73, 97
  skills developed through 97, 100
heating food 62–3
History 31, 49
home
  links with school 75, 76
  role in health education 2
  see also family/home; Family Life Education
hygiene
  food 60–63
  personal *see* Personal Hygiene
hygiene products 83

immunisation **48**
In Service Teachers' Meetings 59
Independence and Leisure
  as component of PSE **5**
  module 1 independence skills/ASDAN
    Award Scheme 101–6
  module 2 leisure activities 106–7
  resources 107–8
  useful addresses 108
independent living skills module (ASDAN
    Transition Challenge) **44**, **102**, **103**, **104**,
    105
Individual Targets for Learning 100
Information Technology **103**

jobs in family 43–4, 46

Keeping Healthy Lunchtime Club 100
kitchen, safety in 64, **64**

leisure activities module 106–7
legislation quiz **116**, **119**
lesbians 24
lesson plan **12**
life cycle, stages of **42–3** *see also* life cycles
    module
life cycles module 24, **25**, 31–2, 48

cross-curricular links to 26, 27, 33
see also life cycle, stages of
lifestyle
    balanced and healthy lifestyle module 91–2
    taking responsibility for 93–4
lighter fuel 20
listening skills, developing 55
low fat foods 69, 70
Lucky Dip staff training activity **116**

MENCAP information pack 107
Makaton 58
male / female differences 26–7
Manchester 3, 71, 73
Manchester City Council 22, 23
Manchester Schools' Council 97
masturbation 24, 28, 34–5
Maths 55, 58, 67, **103**, **105**
meals
    breakfast foods **66**, 66–7
    planning and making 65, 65
media
    hygiene products shown in 83
    influence of 92–3
medicine 15, **16**, 16–18
menstruation *see* periods
methods 6
microwave cooker 63
monitoring 10–12
Muslim culture 32, 60, 87–9

National Curriculum 2, 3, 21, 22, 59, 101, **103**
    see also names of subjects
nurse, school 24

obesity 71
old people **43**
organisation, management and co-ordination
    5–10

PE *see* Physical Education
PMLD *see* profound and multiple learning
    disabilities (PMLD), pupils with
parents and carers 11, 13, 21–2, 37, 75, **82**, 87,
    97
periods
    coping with 27–8
    and privacy 33, 34
personal autonomy module (ASDAN Transition
    Challenge) **44**, **102**, **103**, **104**
personal care module 75, 76, 78–9, 83
personal development module (ASDAN

Transition Challenge) **44**, **102**, **103**, **104**
personal history 49
personal hygiene
    ASDAN Award 76
    careers and personal care 87
    certificates 75–6, **80**, **81**
    as component of PSE 5
    cultural practices 87–9
    dental care **76**, 83, **85**, **86**, 87
    and Environmental Aspects of Health 91
    and food handling 60
    involving parents and carers 75, **82**
    personal care **76**, 78, 83
    showering **76**, 83, **84**
    termly planning sheet 77
    mentioned 32
personal safety
    as component of PSE **5**
    group building activities 51–2
    module 1 stranger danger 52–4
    module 2 getting help 54
    module 3 living with traffic 54–5
pets 40–41
physical disability 2
Physical Education (PE) 57, 58, **77**, 88, 91, 93,
    100
Piper Hill School
    aims and philosophy 3–4
    and Advocacy 95, 97
    development of PSE curriculum 1–13
    and Environmental Aspects of Health
    Education 91
    and Family Life Education 37, 43
    and Food and Nutrition 59, 60, 70–73
    and Health Related Exercise 57
    and Independence and Leisure 101
    information about 2–3
    and Personal Hygiene 75, **76**, 78, **82**, 87
    and Personal Safety 51
    and Sex Education 4, 21, 22, 109–21
    and Substance Use and Misuse 15
planning sheet *see* termly planning sheet
playing safely 55
Police / School Liaison Officer 20, 51
policy *see* school policy
positive self-image module (ASDAN Transition
    Challenge) **44**, **102**, **103**, **104**
prayer, Muslim 87–8
precautions, HIV and AIDS 23
primary health care **47**, 49
primary school 7
privacy *see* public and private module

profound and multiple learning disabilities
(PMLD), pupils with
and ASDAN Transition Challenge 101
Communication Passports 26, 30
and exercise 57
and leisure activities 106
and personal hygiene 78, 79
at Piper Hill School 2
progression 7
puberty 27, 36, 79
public and private module 24, **25**, 32–5
cross-curricular links to 28
puppets see shadow puppets

questionnaire, sex education 109, **110**
results **111**

RE see Religious Education
Record of Achievement 7, 10, 26, 30, 75–6
recreation **103**
refrigerators 62
relationships module 24, **25**, 29–31
cross-curricular links to 26
Religious Education (RE)
and ASDAN Transition Challenge **103**
and Environmental Aspects of Health
Education 91, 94
and Family Life Education 37, 38, **39**, 40,
47, 49
and Sex Education 30
resources
access to 7
advocacy **96**
Environmental Aspects of Health Education
93
Family Life Education **39**, 40, 46, 47, 49, 50
Food and Nutrition 67, 68, 70
Health Related Exercise 58
Independence and Leisure 107–8
Personal Hygiene **77**, 83, 87
Personal Safety 53, 54, 55
Sex Education 21, 26, 27, 28, 29, 30, 31 32,
33, 34, 35
Substance Use and Misuse 15–16, 18, 19, 20
responsibilities
and Environmental Aspects of Health
Education 93–4
for personal hygiene 79
Review Summary Report 10–11
road safety 41, 54–5
roles in family 37, 43–6
rubber gloves 23

SLD *see* severe learning disabilities (SLD),
pupils with
safety
food 60–63
in the kitchen 64, **64**
personal 51–5
rules about medicine 18
School Council 97, **98**
School Development Plan 4
school policy
HIV and AIDS 23
sex education 7, 21
school rules on medicines 17–18
schools, role of 2
Science 7, 33, 48, 55, **77**, **103**, **104**
Sensory 58
self-advocacy *see* Advocacy; self-advocacy
module (ASDAN Transition Challenge)
self-advocacy module (ASDAN Transition
Challenge) **44**, **102**, **103**, **104**
self-awareness 30
self-esteem 15, 21, 24, 26, 51, 95
sensations 35
sensory curriculum 3, 100
sensory disability 2
sensory science 58
severe learning disabilities (SLD), pupils with
1, 2, 30, 101, 106
Sex Education
and confidentiality 22–3
identified as priority at Piper Hill School 4
parental rights of withdrawal 21–2
people who teach 7
policy 7, 21
policy on HIV and AIDS 23
programme *see* Sex Education programme
role of teacher and nurse regarding
contraception 23–4
time available for 7
training for 4, 21, 109–21
using visiting speakers for 22
Sex Education programme
as component of PSE **5**
module 1 body parts 24, **25**, 26–9
module 2 relationships 24, **25**, 29–31
module 3 life cycles 24, **25**, 31–2
module 4 public and private 24, **25**, 32–5
module 5 feelings 24, **25**, 35–6
sexual health 29
sexually transmitted diseases 21, 29 *see also*
AIDS; HIV
sexuality / sexual orientation 24

shadow puppets
  making 15–16
  workshops 78, 92, **116**
showering 75, **76**, 83, **84**, 88
smoking **17**, 18–19, 92
sports **103**, 106–7
staff training 4, 11, 16, 21, 109, **115–21**
Statement of Special Educational Needs 76
stranger danger module 52–4
  cross-curricular links 34, 41
Substance Use and Misuse
  as component of PSE **5**
  module 1 medicines **16**, 16–18
  module 2 smoking and alcohol **17**, 18–19
  module 3 other substances 19–20
  training and development 16
  use of resources 15–16
sugars 71
survey of breakfast foods 66, 67
syringe, finding a 19–20

teachers
  and contraceptive advice 23–4
  and parental rights of withdrawal 22
teenager to adult stage of life cycle **42**
teeth
  care of 75, **76**, 83, **85**, **86**, 87
  decay 71
telephone calls, making 54
temperature requirements for food 61, 62
termly planning sheet

ASDAN Award Scheme **96**
Family Life Education **39**
Personal Hygiene **77**
time 7
toilets
  and privacy 33
  and pupils with PMLD 78
  and washing facilities 88
Toothbrushing Chart 83, **86**
Topic Timetable **10**
toy suppliers 108
traffic *see* road safety
training
  monitoring need for 11
  for Sex Education 4, 21, 109–21
  for Substance Use and Misusse 16
tuck shops 73

vaccination **48**
vegetables 67
video recording 54, 55, 83
videos 19, 20, 27, 28, 29, 30, 31, 34, 36, 47 *see
  also* video recording
visiting speakers 22
vitamins 67–8

wet dreams 27
withdrawal, parental rights of 21–2
Wythenshawe Day Resource Centre 3

Yearly Planning and Review Sheet 10, **11**